Praise for Margo Carroll's Guide to Cycling St. Louis

"Exploring—it's what St. Louisans love to do. Our huge metro area is full of new places to ride and explore. Cycling St. Louis is a must for area cyclists. Great maps and directions—from an experienced cyclist who obviously knows her turf. This comprehensive guide will assist the lifelong cyclist and entice the would-be cyclist to get out and get crankin'!"

— *Steve Tiemann*
St. Louis County Park Ranger

"The creation of St. Louis bike paths and trails has seen explosive growth in recent years. Margo Carroll has painstakingly researched and mapped them all. An extremely useful, and unparalleled guide."

— *Ted Curtis*
Executive Director, Trailnet Inc.

"These wonderful bike paths have been one of the area's best kept secrets—until now! Finally we have a guide."

— *Bev Moore*
Illinois Trails Conservancy

"Cycling St. Louis is a tremendous resource for bike enthusiasts everywhere. Whether you are new to Missouri or have lived here all your life, Margo Carroll offers a fresh look at regional bicycle trails, routes and rides. Inspiring, informative and well researched. Who would have thought there were so many diverse riding opportunities in the area? Mountain bikers, roadies and recreational riders will all discover great places to ride in this incredible book."

— *Deb Ridgway*
MetroBIKE

"If your goal is to explore St. Louis, Margo Carroll has put together a wonderful cycling guide. All you have to do is get on your bike and enjoy."

Sc

D1057794

Other Books in the Show Me Missouri Series

A to Z Missouri: The Dictionary of Missouri Place Names

The Complete Katy Trail Guidebook

The Complete Guide to Bed and Breakfasts,
    Guesthouses & Inns of Missouri

Daytrip Illinois

Daytrip Missouri

Exploring Columbia & Central Missouri

Exploring Missouri Wine Country

Forgotten Missourians Who Made History

Gospels in Glass: Stained Glass Windows in Missouri Churches

Hiking Kansas City

Katy Trail Nature Guide

Missouri Folk Heroes of the 20th Century

Missouri Government: A Concise Survey & Study

Missouri Limestone Select: Rock Climbing & Bouldering Guide

Missouri: The Show Me State

Missouri Quick Fact Book

Show Me Mountain Biking

Show Me Romance

The Missouri Story: A History of the State

Wit & Wisdom of Missouri's Country Editors

The Complete Guide to St. Louis Area Road Rides, Bike Paths, Mountain Biking Trails and Other Two-Wheel Getaways

Ridden, Written & Photographed
By Margo "Dirt Gypsy" Carroll

Illustrations by Bob Bliss

Pebble Publishing, Inc.
Rocheport, Missouri

T his book is the updated, revised, reformatted and all-new second edition to Steve Katz' Guide to Cycling St. Louis. With his permission, Pebble Publishing, Inc. will continue to keep this book up-to-date.

Project support by Pebble Publishing staff: Matthew Cook, Brett Dufur, Tawnee Dufur, Walt Goodman, Pippa Letsky & Tyler Lynch.

Managing Editor: Cynthia Thompson

Photographs by Margo Carroll/M2 Images

Maps by Sabrina West

ISBN 1-891708-11-2 15.95

Pebble Publishing, Inc., P.O. Box 2, Rocheport, MO 65279
Phone: (573) 698-3903 • Fax: (573) 698-3108
E-mail: info@pebblepublishing.com
Online: www.pebblepublishing.com
Visit Our Bookstore in Historic Rocheport, Missouri.

Dedication & Acknowledgments

This book is dedicated to my Mom and Dad for being so wonderful. Their wisdom and love inspire me to enjoy the journey and adventure of each and every day. It is also dedicated to Peggy and Ward for their love and friendship and our continuing quests for adventures.

To all of those people who answered my numerous inquiries, your kindness and helpfulness was much appreciated. I am grateful to the many friends whose encouragement helped to keep me hard at work to finish this project. Thanks to Steve Tiemann, Deb Ridgway and Maurice Williams for your expertise. Thanks to Steve Katz for first publishing this book, and for "passing the torch" by allowing me to update it. This experience has given me many fond memories to look back on. And thanks to Brett Dufur for the opportunity to work on this book and for taking a chance on me. I also appreciate the long hours Cynthia Thompson and Sabrina West spent on the "finishing touches."

A special thanks to Peggy. She drove me around, went on rides with me and stayed up late into the night working on this. Without her wisdom, thoughtfulness, encouragement, support and kindness this project never would have been finished, I thank you.

Preface

Honestly, I can't remember ever not having a bike. I remember as a kid, my brother and I would go out on our little bikes for all-day rides. Our parents supported our adventures and were always concerned for our well-being. Little did they know just how far from home our little one-speed bikes took us! We were lucky. We always returned safe and sound from our rides.

Those rides as a kid showed me just how much fun, excitement, and adventure lay not far from my front door. There's a lot out there, for those interested in discovery, and interested in the journey.

Now, as an adult, I still ride. I still find each bicycle ride an adventure—some rides a little more so than others—but each enjoyable as a great diversion from the routine of a normal day. I still get a kick out of riding my bike. And I just can't seem to get tired of being outdoors and up-close to the sights and smells of nature and the world around me.

My advice to the reader? Sure, riding a bike is good for the body. But it's even better for the mind. Enjoy. Enjoy the sights, the smells. Enjoy the people you meet. Enjoy the sweat. Enjoy the adventure. Let yourself remember the pure joy of riding you felt as a kid.

Enjoy the ride.

Margo

Margo

P.S. Wear your helmet. Always. No exceptions. Think of your helmet as the keys to your bike – you can't 'turn the ignition' until your helmet's on. Keep your maps with you. Look them over before you head out. Bring money for food and a phone call. And be courteous to all you encounter.

Introduction

This guide is written with the general public in mind. There is something for everyone! Sometimes bikers stop riding bikes just because they are bored with their current riding routes. With more than 40 rides in and around the St. Louis area highlighted in this book, you will surely find a new favorite ride. In fact, if you rode a different trail each weekend, this book could fill up 40+ weekends of new adventures to beat the biking blues.

This book has an assortment of rides in a variety of settings, requiring different levels of skill. Some rides are ideal for beginners. Some are great for kids. Some will challenge the occasional rider. A few require the rider to be in very good shape. Just about anyone should be able to find rides they can call their favorites right away. I have also included a few longer road routes that have been the most popular with cyclists in the area.

Many of these bike paths are just a few miles in length. For those who prefer a longer ride, ride to the park. Or, find another destination, like somewhere to eat lunch. With just a little creativity, you could create your own favorite bike route!

Suggestions for the novice, hobbyist, and frequent rider: First, a reminder. Riding is always at your own risk. Just because a ride is in this guide does not give anyone a guarantee of safety. Be aware. Act responsibly. Be safe. Be smart. Road routes are prone to change due to construction, detours, etc. Stay alert.

Okay, now for the rest of it: Take your kids! Most of the multi-use trails and bike paths are highly recommended for families. However, I don't recommend taking kids on any of the on-road rides.

Be comfortable with your bicycle skills, and be familiar with your equipment. If you will be riding on-road, remember that there are more cars out during commuting hours. Early morning is the quietest time to ride. It is very peaceful, and is a great way to start the day.

It is not wise to ever ride alone. Even the most skilled riders have mishaps. As with any strenuous physical exercise, if you're just getting started it's a good idea to check in with your doctor.

Think safety at all times. Even in parks and on paths, be aware of what's going on around you. Ride defensively. Car drivers don't always see cyclists, or realize the speed of a cyclist. Keep groups small for on-road rides. Ride in single file when the shoulder is limited or cars are passing.

How to Use This Guide

Each ride is broken into sections. The sections are described below. At the beginning of each ride description you will find the name of the ride, or its title.

Starting Point: This is where you get on your bike & begin the ride.

Directions to Starting Point: Most directions are given as if departing from St. Louis city. Highway directions are given in north, south, east, and west. Local directions are given in left and right.

Approximate Pedaling Time: The key word here is approximate. A direct ride without stops may be quicker than indicated. A lot of stops along the way will lengthen your ride. Times given are a pretty close guess for the average rider, with an average number of stops.

Distance: Well, this is how far the route is. Note additions/ subtractions for repeated or cut out loops.

Ride Description: This section describes the terrain of the ride. On-road, bike path, multi-use path, gravel path, etc. This is where directions are for routes other than designated paths.

Things to See: You can be the tour guide when you go out with your friends. This section provides historical information and descriptions of points of interest. I hope you will enjoy these interesting facts and discoveries as much as I have.

Hazards: Anything that is a potential danger for the rider on this particular route.

Additional Thoughts: There's a little bit of everything here—from notes about restrooms, to local facilities, to contacts for more information.

Terrain: How hilly or flat is it?

Rating: Ratings are given as 'easy,' 'moderate,' 'moderately difficult,' 'difficult.' These ratings would be from the perspective of a person who rides about once a month.

Pre-Ride Checklist

It's always a good idea to check your bike over before going on a ride. Make sure your equipment is in good working order before you go out. Avoid breakdowns so you can enjoy the ride! Inspect your bicycle for the following:

- Wheels are securely attached, and in proper working order.
- All required reflectors and/or lights are intact.
- Seat is adjusted properly for comfortable riding.
- All nuts and bolts are properly tightened.
- Hand grips are secure.
- Tires have proper pressure and are in good condition without cracks or cuts.
- Brakes are properly adjusted.
- Derailleurs are properly adjusted.
- Chain is in good condition and properly lubricated.
- Pedals and cranks are securely fastened.

If you need assistance or are unsure of the condition of your bicycle, visit an area bike shop. Many stores offer free safety inspections and, if needed, provide expert mechanical repair services for reasonable fees.

Mountain Bike Tips

- Wear a helmet.
- Stay on trail. Don't cut switch back turns.
- Announce yourself loud and clear when overtaking other trail users. Pass on the left.
- Be courteous.
- Don't litter.
- Be alert for obstacles in the trail.
- Take water and food/snack.
- Take insect repellent.
- Stay off muddy trails. Riding in mud is no fun, and can cause severe damage to trails.
- Yield to horses. Give them plenty of room.
- Leave nature as you have found it for others to enjoy.
- Enjoy the journey.

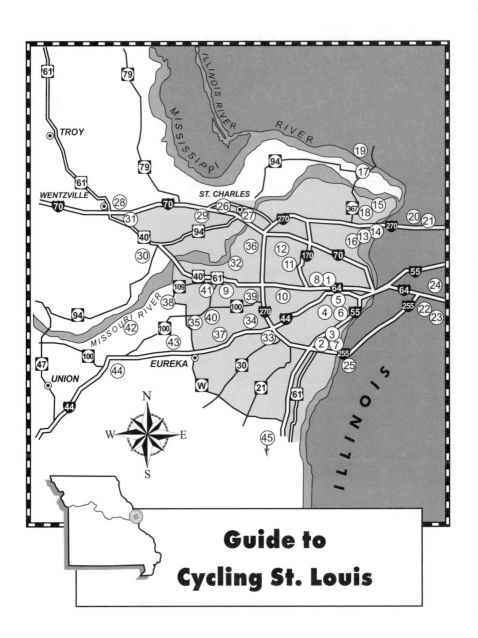

Guide to Cycling St. Louis

CENTRAL

NORTH

ILLINOIS

ST. CHARLES COUNTY

WEST

FAR WEST & BEYOND

CENTRAL

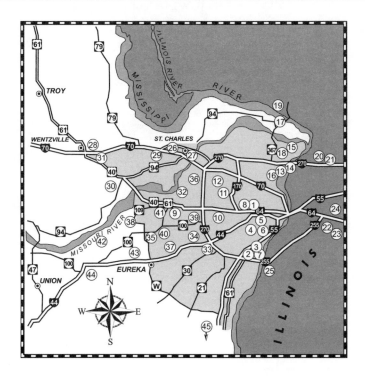

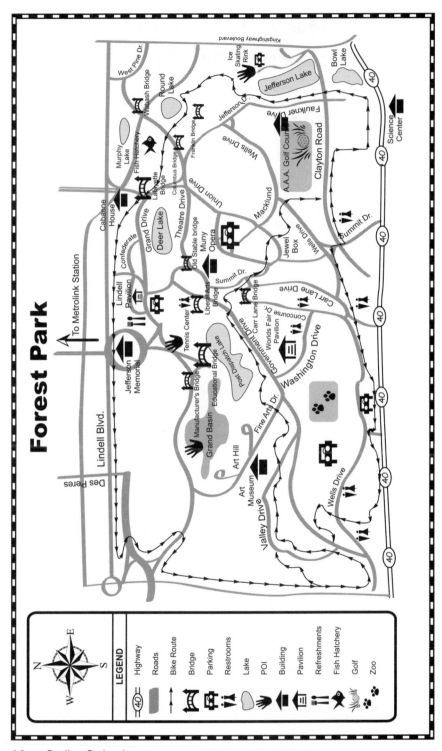

Forest Park Bike Path

Starting Point: Forest Park, St. Louis, Missouri.

Directions to Starting Point: Interstate 64 to Kingshighway north. Make left hand turn into park. There are also entrances to the park off Hampton, Lindell and Skinker. There are several parking lots located around the park including lots by the Muny, Steinberg Rink, the History Museum and at the Art Museum.

Approximate Pedaling Time: 45 minutes to 1½ hour.

Distance: 8.5 miles. (Outer loop 7 miles, Inner loop 1.5 miles).

Ride Description: Paved multi-use path with some hills. This path circles around the large historic park, and has a second smaller inner loop.

Things to See: Forest Park is one of America's largest city parks. The park was purchased for $850,000, and was dedicated in 1876. In 1900 a large portion of the park was cleared in preparation for the 1904 World's Fair. Of the original 1,576 buildings that were constructed for the fair, the ones remaining today are the Art Museum, the Grand Basin, the Bird Cage and a few buildings at Washington

University. In 1911, the U.S. National Championships bicycle race was held in the park. Many more races have been held in the park, including one that went all the way out to Labadie, Missouri. In the 1800s, so many bicyclists frequented the park, that walkers called them "road hogs."

Things to see include the Jewel Box, a wonderful glass building housing plants and seasonal displays; the World's Fair Pavilion, the Art Museum and the History Museum in the Jefferson Memorial. The St. Louis Zoo and the Science Center with the Planetarium are great places to take the kids. Enjoy scenic lake views and wildlife in the park.

Hazards: Bicyclists, walkers, runners and rollerbladers share this trail. It gets very busy.

Additional Thoughts: Drinking water and restrooms are available throughout the park. This is the premiere park in St. Louis and a major tourist attraction. The paved path is an extremely popular place on nice days—a good place for the whole family. Some of the hills may be a bit of a challenge for younger children. Take a picnic lunch for a day-long adventure. There may be an admission fee to some of the park attractions.

Contact Info: City of St. Louis Parks Recreation and Forestry, 5600 Clayton Ave. St. Louis, MO 63110. (314) 289-5300.

Terrain: Mostly flat with a big hill at the Planetarium and another hill along Skinker.

Rating: Moderate.

Be sure to leave time to visit the Saint Louis Art Museum. Its art collection ranges from ancient to contemporary and features masterpieces of Asian art, art of the Renaissance, Impressionism and American Art. The museum, constructed for the 1904 World's Fair, is always free, with an admission only being charged for special exhibitions.

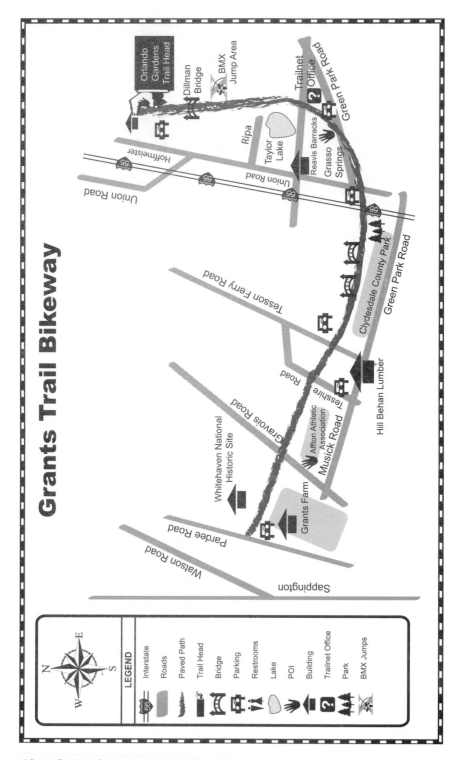

Daniel, Markie and Allison Cerutti out enjoying Grant's Trail.

Grant's Trail Bikeway

Starting Point: South St. Louis County, Missouri.

Directions to Starting Point: There are five parking areas for this bikeway.

Orlando Gardens-Eastern End Trailhead: From I-55 exit at Reavis Barracks Road, go east. Turn left (north) on Union Road. Turn right on to Hoffmeister just before Union goes over I-55, go to Orlando Gardens Banquet Center. Park near the trail on the lower parking lot.

Grasso Spring Trailhead: Exit I-55 at Reavis Barracks Road. Go east one half mile to Green Park Road, turn right, go 100 feet, turn right and park near the trail on the gravel area.

Green Park Trailhead: Exit I-55 at Reavis Barracks Road go east, turn right onto Union Road then right onto Green Park road. Parking area is under I-55.

Hill Behan-Western End Trailhead: Take I-270 to Tesson Ferry Road, go north 2 miles and turn left at the stop light onto Musick

Road. Go 100 feet and turn right onto Tesshire Road. Park adjacent to Hill Behan Lumber by the trail.

Approximate Pedaling Time: 1-2 hours.

Distance: 12.4 miles. (6.2 miles out, 6.2 miles back). Additionally 2.2 miles of the trail remains unpaved. Although unfinished this section of the trail is ridable on a mountain bike.

Ride Description: This rails-to-trails conversion route is flat and paved the entire 6.2 miles.

Things to See: This trail travels along the Gravois Creek and was once a part of the Missouri Pacific railroad. This section of rail eventually made its way to the Mississippi River where the trains crossed on a ferry. Alongside the trail you will find Grasso Springs, a natural spring that feeds a small pond. Taylor Lake is a small lake that was man-made so the owner could have a place to fish. This area is being developed as a wetland area, and the Missouri Department of Conservation will conduct outdoor education classes near Grasso Springs. The trail passes the Historical White Haven Site and Grant's Farm.

Hazards: Nearly 100,000 people visit this trail annually. Hikers, rollerbladers and bicyclists share it. Cars at the crossing of Green Park Road don't have a stop sign. Riders must stop and make sure it is safe to cross. Announce yourself as you pass someone and pass on the left. Occasionally cars do mistakenly drive on the trail.

Additional Thoughts: This is a great place for the whole family. The flat paved trail makes for fun for the kids. The Trailnet office is located on the trail at Reavis Barracks Road. Drinking water is available there. Restrooms are being constructed across from the Trailnet office. Portable restrooms are now available at the Orlando Gardens Trail head and at the area under the I-55 overpass. Stop in the Trailnet office for information on upcoming events and Trailnet T-shirts and souvenirs.

Contact Info: Trailnet Inc., 3900 Reavis Barracks Rd., St. Louis, MO 63125. (314) 416-9930 or (618) 874-8554. E-mail: trailnet@trailnet.org. Website: www.trailnet.org.

Terrain: Flat rail-to-trail conversion bike path.

Rating: Easy.

This is a great place for the whole family. The flat paved trail makes for fun for the kids.

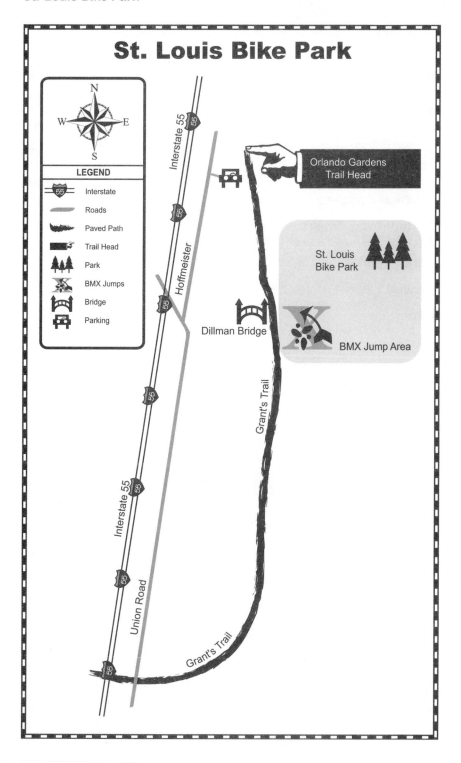

St. Louis Bike Park

Enjoying the wooded, flat trail at St. Louis Bike Park.—Photo by Peggy Welch.

St. Louis Bike Park

Starting Point: Orlando Gardens Trailhead-Grant's Trail.

Directions to Starting Point: From Interstate 55 exit at Reavis Barracks Road, go east. Turn left (north) onto Union Road. Turn right onto Hoffmeister just before Union goes over I-55. Go to Orlando Gardens Banquet Center. Park in the lower half of the Orlando Gardens lot. Enter Grant's Trail trailhead, make a right and follow the paved path. The park is less than 0.8 mile on the left, just after crossing the first bridge (Dillman Bridge).

Distance: Less than 2 miles.

Ride Description: The St. Louis Bike Park consists of an area of BMX jumps and a few mountain bike trails. Trailnet opened the area in 1997 as a "family" area so that everyone can enjoy the trails. The area is flat and the trails curve around through the wooded area. The BMX area is the place to go to sharpen your jumping skills. The area has several large jumps and some rhythm sections that are great for those into dirt jumping and BMX.

Things to See: The thing to see is the "big air" of riders on the jumps. Wildlife is also attracted to the wooded area and the creek. Lots of birds dart about.

Hazard: This area can get very muddy. "Big air" means big crashes. Wear a helmet! Take bug spray and watch for slick mud spots. The trails are not clearly marked.

Additional Thoughts: Don't expect an epic trail ride. This is a good place to practice your off-road biking skills and maybe take the kids so they can ride on flat dirt trails and the BMX jumps. This area continues to evolve.

Contact Info: Trailnet, Inc., 3900 Reavis Barracks, St. Louis, MO 63125. (314) 416-9930 or (618) 874-8554. E-mail: Trailnet@trailnet.org. Website: www.trailnet.org.

Terrain: Flat.

Rating: Easy. The jumps are challenging!

Notes:

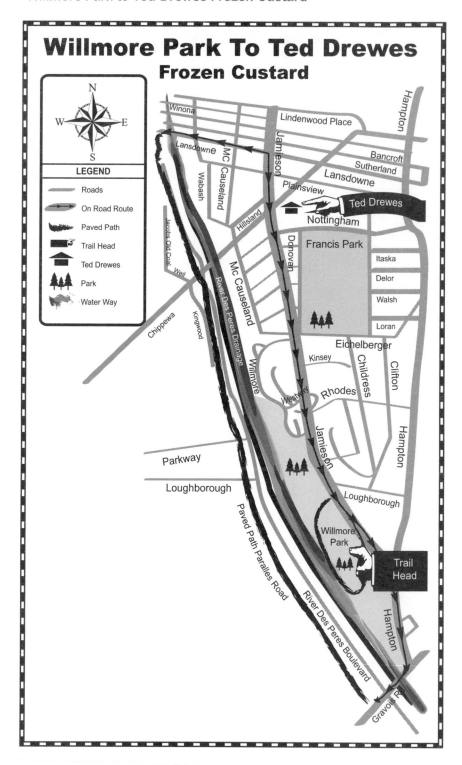

Willmore Park is one of the city's most popular parks, providing large areas of open land.

Willmore Park to Ted Drewes Frozen Custard

Starting Point: Willmore Park, St. Louis, Missouri.

Directions to Starting Point: From St. Louis take Interstate 44 west to the Arsenal exit. Turn right onto Arsenal. Turn left on Jamieson. Stay on Jamieson past Chippewa. Willmore Park will be on the right.

Approximate Pedaling Time: 1-2 hours.

Distance: 7 miles.

Ride Description: On-road and bike paths. First, you can explore the park on the bike paths in the park. The paths are all paved and intertwine between the two lakes, the playground and the picnic areas. From there exit the park and take Jamieson Road north. At Chippewa turn RIGHT to a stop for a custard treat at Ted Drewes. Next, go back on Chippewa and turn RIGHT on Jamieson. Turn LEFT on Lansdowne. At the intersection of Lansdowne and River Des Peres Boulevard look for the bike path that runs parallel with River Des Peres Blvd. opposite the River Des Peres Drainage River. Travel on the bike path south to where it ends at Gravois. Turn LEFT on Gravois.

Cross the River Des Peres Drainage River, turn LEFT on Hampton. Follow Hampton to Jamieson back to the park.

Things to See: This park was developed in 1947, thanks to the generous gift of Cyrus Crane Willmore, a prominent real estate developer. The park has several playgrounds and ballfields. On this ride, be sure and treat yourself at Ted Drewes Frozen Custard, a St. Louis landmark, opened in 1929. A great treat on a warm summer day. Chippewa is part of the Historic Route 66 Highway.

Hazards: Traffic, road hazards, holes, debris on the roadway. The bike path along River Des Peres is in bad shape in a few spots with holes and rough areas. Watch for traffic at street crossings. There are several crossings.

Additional Thoughts: There are drinking fountains and restrooms at Willmore Park. There are several picnic shelters and picnic areas. The paved trails in Willmore Park are good for the kids.

Contact Info: City of St. Louis Parks Recreation and Forestry, 5600 Clayton Ave. St. Louis, MO 63110. (314) 289-5300.

Terrain: Flat with a few small hills.

Rating: Moderate.

Bicycle Trail Sign at Willmore Park.

Deb Ridgway on a city ride.

MetroBIKE

Did you know that many trips under 3 miles are faster by bicycle? That's right, and that's the message MetroBIKE is working hard to spread. MetroBIKE, a project of Trailnet Inc., through planning, advocacy and educational programs in the St. Louis area, is working to make our community more bicycle-friendly and more aware of using bicycles for transportation. How about riding your bike to work, up to the grocery store or to the mailbox?

Their projects include promoting road sharing safety education for motorists and bicyclists, encouraging local governments to adopt bicycle-safe transportation policies that will make it easier and safer for us to use our bicycles to go places instead of jumping into our cars, and to build a cycling constituency.

MetroBIKE's
Basics of On-road Bicycle Safety Tips

Motorists and cyclists have a legal right to all roads in most areas. This doesn't necessarily mean, though, that all motorists are aware of these rights.

- As a general rule, bicyclists must obey the same traffic laws as vehicle drivers.

- Always ride with the traffic flow, as close to the right edge of the road as is safe.

- Obey all traffic signals, signs and pavement markings.

- Wear a helmet. Don't ride without a properly-fit helmet.

- Be courteous.

- Plan your route.

- Use hand signals. Hand signals advise motorists and pedestrians of your intentions.

- Be visible. Never assume that the drivers around you have seen you. Wear reflective clothing. Make sure your bike is equipped with the proper lights and reflectors if you are going to be riding at night. The Missouri State Statutes Regarding Bicycling states that any bicycle used on the street a half hour after sunset must be equipped with a front-facing white light visible from 500 feet and a red rear light (or reflector) with a width of two square inches visible from 600 feet. Reflective material must be visible on each side of the bike or bicyclist, visible from 300 feet and reflective material must be visible from 200 feet from the front and rear of a bicyclist's pedals, shoes or lower legs.

- Parked cars. Watch for opening car doors or cars pulling away without signaling. Don't weave in between parked cars. Be alert at alley openings and side streets.

- Dogs. Try voicing a firm command, such as "Stay!" Carrying spray protection, such as "Halt!" can be an effective last resort.

- Headphones. Although not prohibited by law, headphones are not safe to use while bicycling. Headphones block sounds that a cyclist should hear (emergency vehicles, etc.) and puts you at risk for accidents and injuries.

- Carry tools with you at all times to repair a flat or make adjustments.

- Bad weather. Pavement will be slick in rain, especially the painted stripes. Pay attention, brakes work differently in wet weather.

These tips are guidelines for making your ride more enjoyable and safe. For more information on these and other MetroBIKE efforts, Trailnet may be contacted at (314) 416-9930.

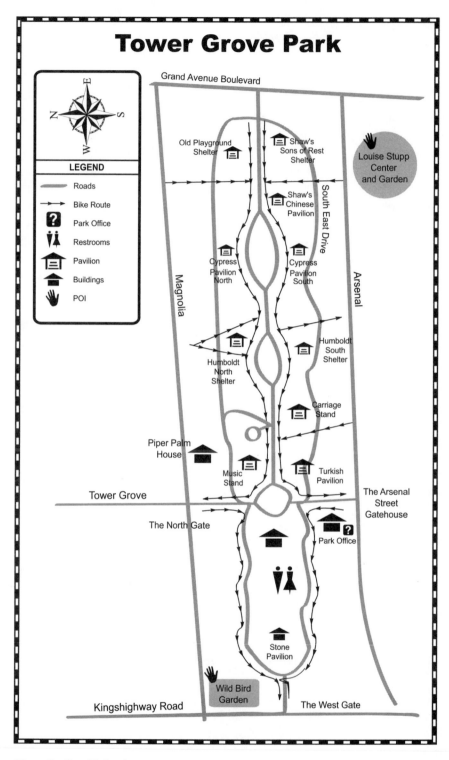

Tower Grove Park

Grand Avenue Boulevard

LEGEND

Roads
Bike Route
Park Office
Restrooms
Pavilion
Buildings
POI

Old Playground Shelter

Shaw's Sons of Rest Shelter

Louise Stupp Center and Garden

Shaw's Chinese Pavilion

South East Drive

Cypress Pavilion North

Cypress Pavilion South

Magnolia

Arsenal

Humboldt South Shelter

Humboldt North Shelter

Carriage Stand

Piper Palm House

Music Stand

Turkish Pavilion

Tower Grove

The Arsenal Street Gatehouse

The North Gate

Park Office

Stone Pavilion

Wild Bird Garden

Kingshighway Road

The West Gate

The multi-use path at Tower Grove Park curves among large trees and ornate pavilions.

Tower Grove Park

Starting Point: Tower Grove Park, St. Louis, Missouri.

Directions to Starting Point: From Interstate 44, exit Kingshighway South. The park entrance will be on the left. Large white stone pillars line the entrance. Park along the road in parking areas.

Approximate Pedaling Time: 45 minutes.

Distance: 4-mile loop.

Ride Description: This is a paved multi-use path shared by bicyclists and others. The path curves among large trees and ornate pavilions. There are 10 ornately painted and designed pavilions in the park.

Things to See: This 19th century Victorian park is a National Historic Landmark, designed, built and donated to the city by Henry Shaw. Its 289 acres feature colorful pavilions, fountains and lily pools. Shaw Botanical Gardens is just a few blocks away. The colorful pavilions date back to the 1800s. The ruins around the pond are from the remains of the Lindell Hotel, which burned in 1867. Henry Shaw planted most of the trees.

Hazards: Use caution when crossing roadways.

Additional Thoughts: The paved loop trail around the park is a good place to take the kids to ride, but use caution at the road crossings. By taking a short ride up to South Grand you can pick up lunch at the South City Diner (3141 S. Grand). A&M Cyclery is adjacent to the park at 4282 Arsenal, should you need any supplies or repairs.

Contact Info: City of St. Louis Parks, Recreation & Forestry, 5600 Clayton Ave. St. Louis, MO 63110. (314) 289-5300.

Terrain: Paved trail. Mostly flat. Small hills.

Rating: Easy.

Tower Grove Park's mist-filled Main Street. Opposite page: Tower Grove Park's Music Stand.

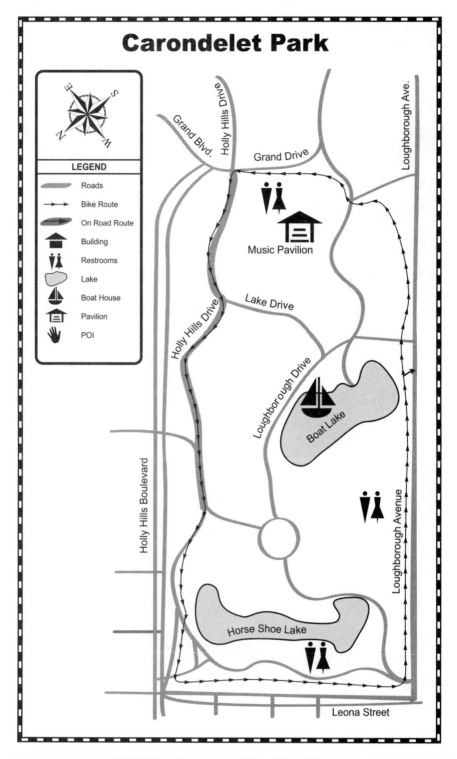

Carondelet Park

Horse Shoe Lake is one of two lakes in Carondelet Park
formed by enlarging and connecting former sinkholes.

Carondelet Park

Starting Point: Carondelet Park, St. Louis, Missouri.

Directions to Starting Point: From Interstate 55, exit at the Loughborough exit. Go west on Loughborough Avenue. Go a short distance and turn right onto Loughborough Drive, follow into the park. Street parking is allowed in the park. You can get onto the trail where it crosses Loughborough Drive.

Approximate Pedaling Time: 20 minutes.

Distance: 1.8-mile loop.

Ride Description: This is a paved trail around the park with a short 0.6-mile section on Holly Hills Drive, one of the park roads. The route has a few small hills and passes two lakes and many sinkholes.

Things to See: The park was dedicated on July 4th, 1876, and was named in honor of Frenchman Baron Francois Louis Hector de Carondelet, the Spanish Governor of Louisiana. The park has a very interesting collection of sinkholes. The two lakes were made by enlarging and connecting former sinkholes. Nearly 20 sinkholes dot the park's landscape. Sinkholes are formed when dissolving limestone creates underground chambers, which then collapse.

Above, Horse Shoe Lake at Carondelet Park. To the left, Carondelet Park's Music Pavilion.

There are several interesting buildings in the park: The Boat House built in 1918, the Music Pavilion built in 1898 and the Music Stand built in 1898.

Hazards: Watch for vehicles when crossing roads.

Additional Thoughts: This picturesque park, with its lakes and wonderful huge pine trees, makes for a great escape from the city. The paved trail is a good place for the kids to ride. Drinking water and restrooms are available at the park. Fishing is permitted with the proper Missouri fishing license.

Carondelet's
Horse Shoe
Lake Bike Path.

Contact Info: City of St. Louis Parks Recreation and Forestry, 5600 Clayton Ave. St. Louis, MO 63110. (314) 289-5300.

Terrain: Small rolling hills.

Rating: Easy.

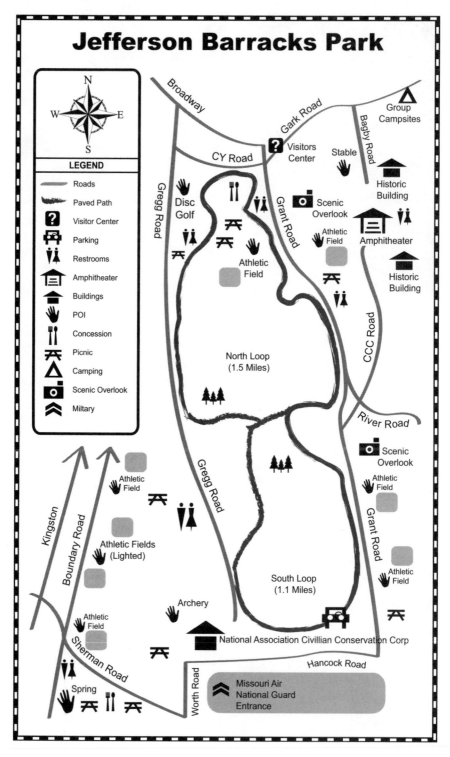

Jefferson Barracks was the first "permanent base"
west of the Mississippi to house troops.

Jefferson Barracks Park

Starting Point: South St. Louis County, Missouri.

Directions to Starting Point: Take Interstate 270 (255) south to the Telegraph Road exit north. Stay to the right onto Kingston and continue on to South Broadway. Turn right onto South Broadway into the park.

Approximate Pedaling Time: 20 minutes a lap.

Distance: 2.7-mile asphalt paved trail. The North Loop is 1.5 miles, the South Loop is 1.1 miles. (The outer perimeter of both loops is 2.4 miles). Some people prefer to ride the roads through the park, that loop is about 3 miles.

Ride Description: Paved multi-use trail. This bicycle path consists of two loops that are in the shape of a figure 8. The paths have some hills and travel through a prairie area and forest areas.

Things to See: Jefferson Barracks was established in 1826 as the site for the first Infantry School of Practice in the United States. The land was acquired from the village of Carondelet for $5. It was to serve as the primary training and gathering place for the Army of the

Be sure and visit the Jefferson Barracks scenic overlook
where you can see the Mississippi River.

West. The red brick barracks buildings are visible from the south loop. Historic buildings which house museums are: the limestone, fortress-like "Ordnance room" and the "Powder Magazine" buildings. The iron fence is made from Civil War-era rifle barrels.

In 1950, St. Louis County acquired 420 acres of Barracks land for a park. The military reservation sits on high ground, overlooking the Mississippi River. Scenic Circle Drive leads to the overlook of the Mississippi. In 1972, Jefferson Barracks was placed on the National Register of Historic Places.

Hazards: The trail can get busy with other trail users. Watch out for dogs. Use caution at road crossings.

Additional Thoughts: Restrooms and drinking water are available at both ends of the bike paths at the parking areas. This paved trail is a good place to take the kids on a bike ride. At one time there was a concession stand on the north loop, but it is now closed and only a soda machine is available.

Contact Info: St. Louis County Parks, 41 S. Central Ave., Clayton, MO 63105. (314) 615-7275 (PARK).

Rating: Easy.

The Jefferson Barracks paved trail is a good place to take the kids on a ride.
Try to plan your visit at off-peak times to avoid the crowd.

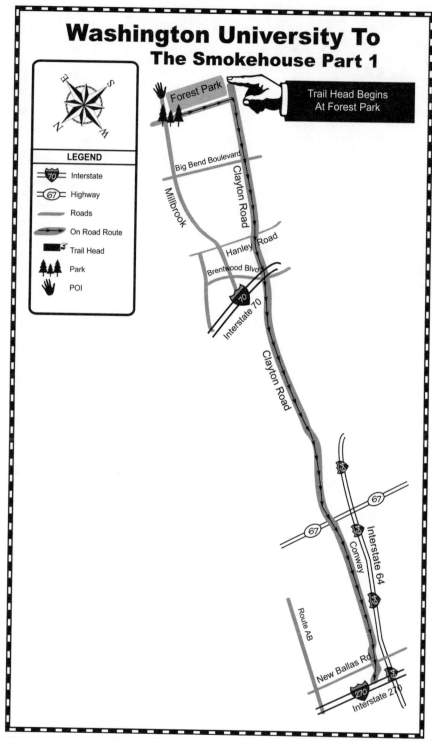

Washington University To
The Smokehouse Part 1

Trail Head Begins
At Forest Park

Forest Park

Big Bend Boulevard

Clayton Road

Millbrook

Hanley Road

Brentwood Blvd

Interstate 70

Clayton Road

Conway

Interstate 64

Route AB

New Ballas Rd

Interstate 270

LEGEND

70	Interstate
67	Highway
	Roads
	On Road Route
	Trail Head
	Park
	POI

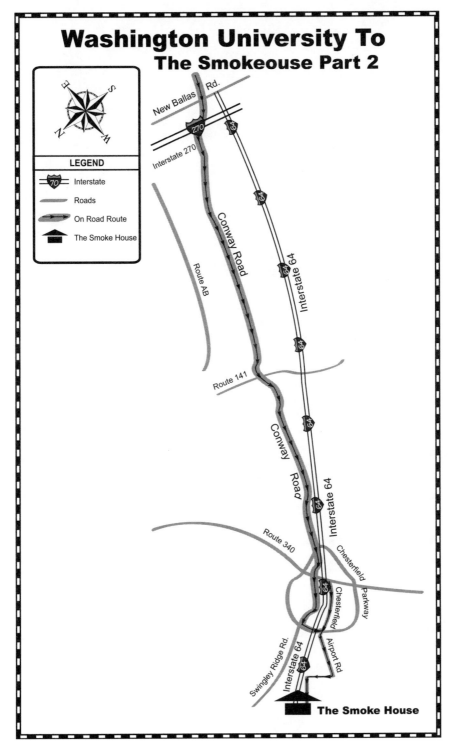

Washington University To
The Smokeouse Part 2

LEGEND

- Interstate
- Roads
- On Road Route
- The Smoke House

New Ballas Rd.

270

64

Interstate 270

Conway Road

Route AB

Interstate 64

Route 141

Conway Road

Interstate 64

Route 340

Chesterfield Parkway

Chesterfield

Swingley Ridge Rd.

Interstate 64

Airport Rd

The Smoke House

The Washington University/Forest Park to the Smoke House ride goes through the central corridor of St. Louis, which was home to numerous country clubs in the mid 1920s.—Photo by Peggy Welch.

Washington University– Forest Park to the Smoke House

Starting Point: Washington U. – Forest Park, St. Louis, Missouri.

Directions to Starting Point: From St. Louis take Interstate 64/40 west to Clayton Road exit. Take Clayton Road to Skinker, turn right. You can park at Washington University or at Forest Park.

Approximate Pedaling Time: 2-4 hours.

Distance: 36 miles. (18 miles out, 18 miles back).

Ride Description: This is an on-road ride that starts at Washington University/Forest Park. Cycle out to Skinker and go south to Clayton Road. Turn Right (west) on Clayton Road. You will pass the Esquire Theater and Panera Bread. Stop for something to eat if you want. Continue on Clayton Road west. Just after Ladue Junior High School, turn RIGHT onto Conway. Turn LEFT onto Lindbergh for just a short distance, then RIGHT onto Conway. Continue on Conway, cross Chesterfield Parkway. Turn LEFT onto Swingley Ridge. Continue on Swingley Ridge past Olive. Turn LEFT onto Chesterfield Parkway West. Turn RIGHT onto Chesterfield Airport. Turn RIGHT onto Baxter Rd. for a short distance. Then turn LEFT back onto Chesterfield Airport to the Smokehouse on the left. Return the same way.

Things to See: This ride goes through the central corridor of St. Louis, which was home to numerous country clubs in the mid 1920s Stringent zoning laws were established by the environmentally minded owners of the country clubs in order to control the expansion of commercial and industrial use in the area and to establish large 1.8- to 3-acre home site lot requirements along Clayton Road. Before 1830, Clayton Road was a trail called Fox Creek Road. Busch's Grove Restaurant, at 9160 Clayton Road, was built in the late 1850s and at one time was a stage coach stop.

Hazards: Road hazards such as holes, gravel on road, and vehicles.

Additional Thoughts: This route is used by many cyclists. Bike shops are just south on Big Bend at the intersection of Clayton Road.

Terrain: Large rolling hills, with a few steep hills.

Rating: Difficult.

Photo by Peggy Welch.

Mark Twain once said, "It's better to travel than to arrive."
He obviously didn't know about Smoke House Market, where cyclists
have been known to gather, eat, and sometimes forget all about the ride.

The Smoke House Market

The Smoke House Market is the meeting place for cyclists in the St. Louis area. On any given day, at nearly any time of the day, you will see cyclists gathering there, getting ready for a ride or just getting finished with one. Situated in the Missouri River Bottoms, the Smoke House stands as a brick landmark for cyclists.

Built back in 1937, it was originally named the Chesterfield Mercantile and was owned by Andrew and Lela Kroeger. Even back in those days, cyclists passed by on the annual Bellefontaine Bicycle Road Race of the St. Louis Cycling Club (which originated back in 1906). The business and property were sold in 1952 to Frank and Claire Wiegand.

The Wiegands named the store the Smoke House Market and operated it for more than 30 years before selling it in 1986 to their daughter Jane.

Today Jane and her husband Thom continue running the business and Annie Gunn's Restaurant. The market and restaurant are well known for their fine food and wonderful selection of wines.

Many cyclists were attracted to the low amounts of traffic on the flat roads and scenic hilly roads. This is changing, though. With the building boom in this area, much more traffic travels these scenic backroads than has in the past.

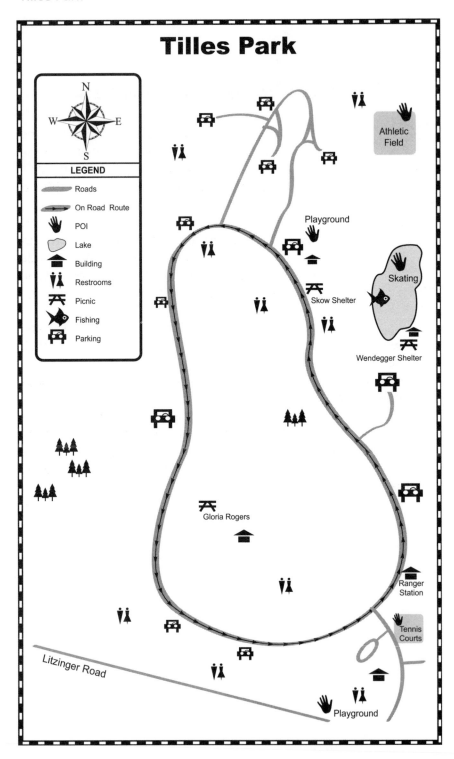

Tilles Park

LEGEND

Roads
On Road Route
POI
Lake
Building
Restrooms
Picnic
Fishing
Parking

Athletic Field

Playground

Skating

Skow Shelter

Wendegger Shelter

Gloria Rogers

Ranger Station

Tennis Courts

Litzinger Road

Playground

Tilles Park

Starting Point: Tilles Park, Ladue, Missouri.

Directions to Starting Point: From St. Louis take Interstate 64/40 west to the McKnight Road Exit south. Take McKnight south. The park will be on the right just before Litzinger Road.

Approximate Pedaling Time: 10 minutes a lap.

Distance: 1 mile.

Ride Description: This is an on-road route. The park road loops around the park for a one-mile mostly flat route.

Things to See: This is a nice wooded urban park. Although this is a short course it is a good escape from most of the urban traffic. Mornings are fairly quiet with low traffic.

Hazards: Road hazards such as traffic, pedestrians, holes, and debris on the roadway.

Additional Thoughts: The wooded park offers fishing, playgrounds, picnicking, and ballfields. Drinking water and restrooms are available at the park.

Contact Info: St. Louis County Parks, 41 S. Central Ave., Clayton, MO 63105. (314) 615-7275 (PARK).

Terrain: Mostly flat with a few very small hills.

Rating: Easy.

Tilles Park is a nice wooded urban park that offers an escape from most urban traffic.

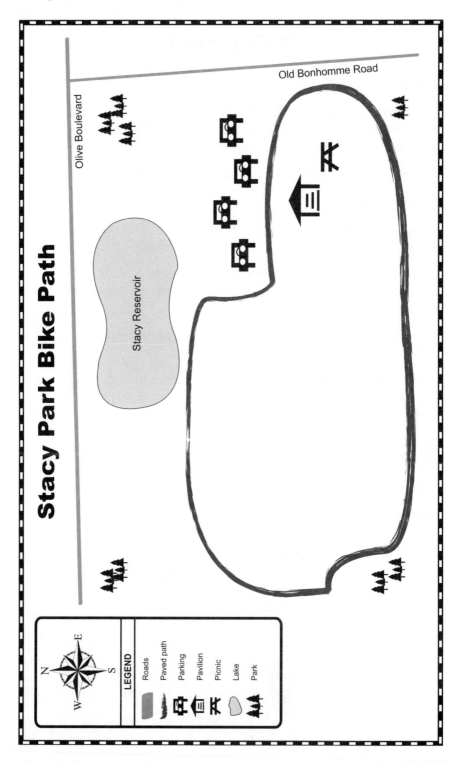

Stacy Park Bike Path

Old Bonhomme Road

Olive Boulevard

Stacy Reservoir

LEGEND

Roads
Paved path
Parking
Pavilion
Picnic
Lake
Park

N E S W

Stacy Park Bike Path

Starting Point: Olivette, Missouri.

Directions to Starting Point: From I-270 take Olive Blvd. east. Turn right on Old Bonhomme Road. The park will be on the right.

Approximate Pedaling Time: 10-15 minutes a lap.

Distance: 0.7-mile loop.

Ride Description: Paved multi-use trail. Bicyclist, walkers, runners and rollerbladers share this paved path. The path loops around the perimeter of the park.

Things to See: The prairie area is just a short walk from the paved path on the north side of the park. The Stacy Reservoir sits on the north side of the park. This reservoir was built by the City of St. Louis in 1926. The construction was unique in that instead of digging a large hole for the reservoir, cement walls were built and then the dirt was filled in around the walls by using a conveyor belt powered by a tractor. Water from the reservoir was carried to the city in large underground pipes.

Hazards: Watch for other trail users and dogs.

Additional Thoughts: Although this trail is short, it makes a great place to get away for a nice ride. Drinking water and restrooms are available at the park. There are several picnic areas, a pavilion, and ballfields to enjoy at the park, as well as Bar-B-Q pits.

Contact Info: Olivette Parks and Recreation, 9723 Grandview Drive, Olivette, MO 63132. (314) 991-1249.

Terrain: Flat paved trail.

Rating: Easy.

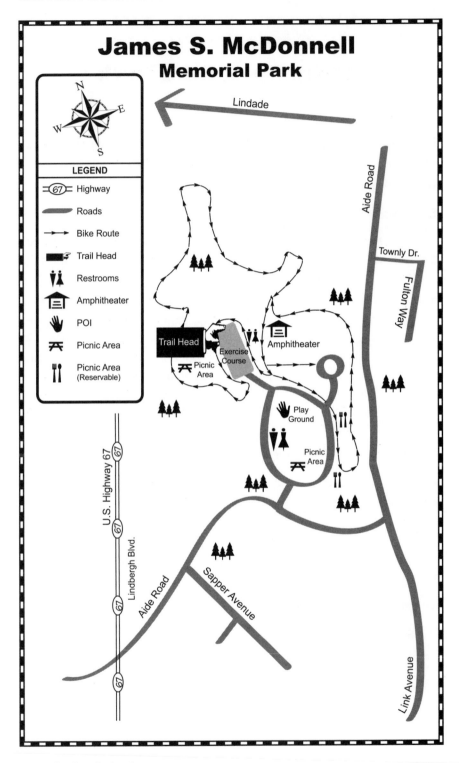

James S. McDonnell
Memorial Park

LEGEND

- 67 Highway
- Roads
- Bike Route
- Trail Head
- Restrooms
- Amphitheater
- POI
- Picnic Area
- Picnic Area (Reservable)

Lindade

Aide Road

Townly Dr.

Fulton Way

Trail Head

Exercise Course

Amphitheater

Picnic Area

Play Ground

Picnic Area

U.S. Highway 67

Lindbergh Blvd.

Aide Road

Sapper Avenue

Link Avenue

The paved, multi-use trail at this park makes for a nice little ride.
It is a good place to take children.

James S. McDonnell Memorial Park

Starting Point: James S. McDonnell Memorial Park, St. Ann, Missouri.

Directions to Starting Point: From Interstate 270 take Page Ave. east. Take Lindberg north, turn right on Adie. Follow Adie and the park entrance will be on the left.

Approximate Pedaling Time: 10 minutes per lap.

Distance: 1.3 miles.

Ride Description: This is a paved multi-use trail. The trail loops around the wooded park.

Things to See: This small wooded urban park attracts birds and other wildlife. The picnic area, Bar-B-Q pit, playground, sand volleyball court, and amphitheater provide other opportunities for family fun.

Hazards: Use caution at road crossings.

Additional Thoughts: Much of this park is still undeveloped on the other side of Adie Road. The paved trail makes a nice little ride, good to take the kids. Drinking water and restrooms are available at the park.

Contact Info: St. Louis County Parks, 41 S. Central Ave., Clayton, MO 63105. (314) 615-7275 (PARK).

Terrain: Small hills.

Rating: Easy.

NORTH

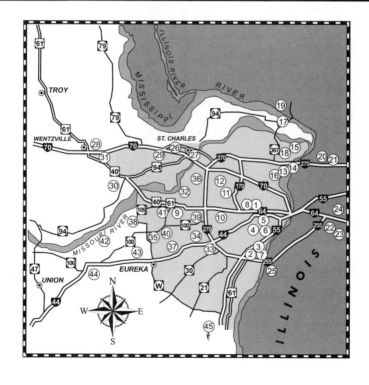

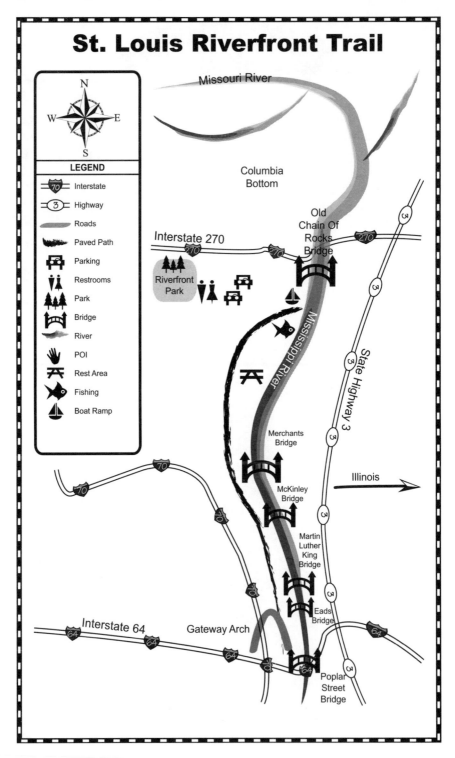

St. Louis Riverfront Trail

St. Louis Riverfront Trail

Starting Point: North Riverview Park, St. Louis, Missouri.

Directions to Starting Point: From North County take Interstate 270 to Riverview Drive South. Trailhead is at the south end of the park, at the second parking area, about 2.8 miles from I-270.

Approximate Pedaling Time: 2-3 hours.

Distance: 24 miles. (12 miles out, 12 miles back).

Ride Description: Paved multi-use trail. The Riverfront Trail starts in North Riverview Park and travels along the riverfront to Laclede's Landing, near the Gateway Arch. This greenway runs along the shores of the Mississippi with terrific views of the river and a view of the city that is rarely seen. The trail crosses over the levee and runs between the river and the flood walls a lot of the way.

Things to See: It's amazing to see the amount of wildlife along this city greenway. Bald Eagles, fox, squirrels and rabbits are common sights. The trail passes the Street Department's storage area that houses old paving stones once used to pave the streets of St. Louis. Watch the boat traffic on the river and see the large Mosenthein

Island. Observe the native plant restoration areas. Eagle viewing is best from December through February.

Hazards: Take water. It isn't always available along the trail. The Coast Guard Building rest area is currently open Tuesday through Friday 7 a.m. to 7 p.m. and Saturday & Sunday 9 a.m. to 5 p.m. Rest room and water are available. The trail can, at times, be flooded. This trail is somewhat isolated.

Additional Thoughts: This is one of the areas most visual trails, with views of the Mississippi River and St. Louis. Restrooms are located at the parking lot in North Riverview Park. You will pass the "Old" Chain of Rocks Bridge just before entering North Riverview Park. Some day the Chain of Rocks Bridge will connect to the Riverfront Trail and link the trails in Illinois and Missouri. The trail is closed 10 p.m. to 6 a.m.

Contact Info: Trailnet Inc., 3900 Reavis Barracks, St. Louis, MO 63125. (314) 416-9930 or (618) 874-8554. E-mail: Trailnet@trailnet.org. Website: www.trailnet.org.

Terrain: Flat and paved.

Rating: Moderate.

The trail runs between the river and the flood walls much of the way,
and offers terrific views of the river, and a view of the city that is rarely seen.

Trailnet Inc.

Trailnet is a not-for-profit land trust that plans, promotes and implements multi-use trails and greenways and encourages bicycle transportation. The organization boasts more than 2,000 members and has obtained federal funding for bikeways and greenways in the St. Louis area. Trailnet was instrumental with the development of the Riverfront Trail, Grant's Trail, the Chain of Rocks Bridge rehabilitation and the Confluence Greenway project.

They rely on memberships, volunteers, donations and fund raising events to make these projects happen. They can be contacted at: Trailnet Inc., 3900 Reavis Barracks Road, St. Louis, MO 63125. (314) 416-9930. Send e-mail to: trailnet@trailnet.org. Or visit their website at: www.trailnet.org.

Where's the drawbridge? These aren't castles from Ireland—they're remnants of Missouri's days of architectural grandeur. These intake towers can easily be seen from the Old Chain of Rocks Bridge.

The Old Chain of Rocks Bridge is now a multi-use path that spans the Mississippi River. It is closed to automobile traffic, making it the perfect place for a short ride, a leisurely stroll or the perfect perch for migratory bird watching.

Old Chain of Rocks Bridge

Directions to Starting Point: From the Missouri side: Interstate 270 north to the last Missouri exit—Exit 34—River View Drive South. After approximately one-quarter of a mile you will see the bridge on the left. The bridge is fenced off. From the Illinois side: Interstate 270 west to Illinois Rt.. 3 south. At first stop light turn right on Chain of Rocks Road, continue for about a mile. You will cross the Chain of Rocks Canal bridge (steel deck), and the Chain of Rocks Bridge will be straight ahead. The road is closed to the bridge.

Approximate Pedaling Time: The Old Chain of Rocks Bridge is open daily (including holidays) one-half hour before sunrise to one-half hour after sunset daily. These hours may change after May 31, 2003. Call the Trailnet office for the most up-to-date times or check out their web site for special event dates.

Distance: The bridge is almost one mile long (5,353 feet).

Things to See: Great views of the Mississippi River, the skyline of St. Louis, the castle-like water intake towers. Peregrine falcons frequently visit the bridge to eat their catch. Wintering eagles can be seen in the trees and hunting between December and March.

Contact Info: Trailnet Inc., 3900 Reavis Barracks, St. Louis, MO 63125. (314) 416-9930 or (618) 874-8554. Trailnet@trailnet.org. www.trailnet.org.

The Old Chain of Rocks Bridge:
Bridge of Many Uses and Many Dreams

The term "Chain of Rocks" refers to the natural section of rocks that form a ridge across the Mississippi River just south of the bridge. This section of river was treacherous for boat navigation. The Chain of Rocks Canal was built in 1952 so that boat traffic could avoid this section of the river.

The Old Chain of Rocks Bridge was the fifth bridge across the Mississippi River near St. Louis. Construction began in 1927 and was expected to only take a year, but due to bad weather and flooding the construction took nearly two years at a cost of $2,000,000.

On June 25th, 1928, John Scott, the owner/promoter of the toll bridge, anxiously opened the bridge two hours early. Ornate tollbooths and a park-like setting surrounded the bridge.

In 1936 it became part of the famous Route 66 highway system that connected Chicago to the Pacific Ocean.

Stricter federal regulations in 1939 that cut profits for private bridge operators forced the Kingshighway Bridge Company, the

A painted marker serves as a faded reminder of the bridge's historic past. In 1936 it became part of the famous Route 66 highway system that connected Chicago to the Pacific Ocean.

Be sure and visit the old Chain of Rocks Bridge multi-use path for its history, its view of the St. Louis skyline and its view of the Mississippi River.

original owners, to sell the bridge to the City of Madison, Illinois for $2,300,000.

The City of Madison, the present owner of the bridge, continued to operate the toll bridge until 1967. The bridge closed in 1968.

There were several "creative" ideas over the years for using the bridge, including an idea from the army to use the bridge for demolition practice and blow it up.

The bridge sat still and unused for 28 years. In 1987, Trailnet Inc., began work on a plan that would reopen the bridge. The plan is a vision of greenways and trails along the Mississippi River on both the Missouri and Illinois sides.

The Chain of Rocks Bridge will provide the key link between the greenways, and has becoming quite a tourist attraction. Trailnet holds several public events on the bridge such as moonlight walks, an annual birthday party (June 25th), eagle viewing days, bike rides across the river and various other events.

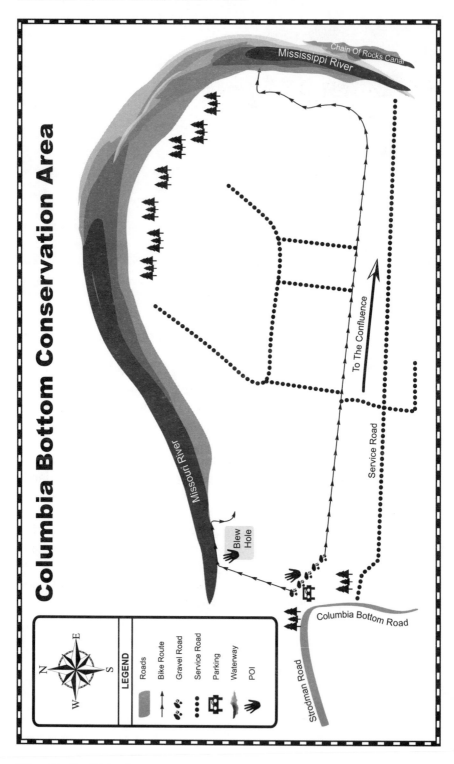

Peggy Welch enjoying the view.

Columbia Bottom Conservation Area Mountain Bike Trail

Starting Point: Columbia Bottom Conservation Area in north St. Louis County.

Directions to Starting Point: Take Interstate 270 to the Riverview Drive exit (the last exit before crossing into Illinois). Go north 3 miles on Riverview Drive (Columbia Bottom Road), the gravel parking area will be straight ahead at the intersection with Strodman Road.

Approximate Pedaling Time: 1-2 hours.

Distance: 8 miles round trip. (4 miles out, 4 miles back).

Ride Description: Multi-use dirt trail. The trail is a dirt farm road that goes out four miles to the confluence of the Missouri and Mississippi Rivers. As you get closer to the river you will cross over a levee, the trail narrows as you get closer to the confluence. Sections of the trail near the rivers can at times be flooded, very muddy and difficult to follow.

The Columbia Bottom Mountain Biking Trail is marked with white signs.

Things to See: The view of the confluence of the Mississippi and the Missouri Rivers is the main attraction to this ride. You can actually see the two different colors of the river waters coming together. Most of the area between the trailhead and the river is cropland. Herons and egrets are common along the shoreline and in the wetland areas. There are beautiful wildflowers in the summer. This is a great place for bird watching, so take the binoculars!

Hazards: The area is prone to occasional flooding. A muddy condition near the confluence is common. Hunting is permitted only during special hunts or by holders of a valid daily hunting permit. Check with the Department of Conservation for specific days when hunting is allowed.

Additional Thoughts: The 4,318 acres of river bottomlands were opened by the Department of Conservation in 1998. This area is in the planning stages for future recreational use, improvements, and additions. These developments will include shallow wetlands, bottomland forests, and bottomland prairies. There is no water available and only a porta-potty for restroom facilities. Take plenty of water and bug spray. The trail is marked with white signs. There's also another short trail out to some blew holes by the river. The area is closed from 10 p.m. to 6 a.m. daily from April 1 to September 30 and from 7 p.m. to 6 a.m. daily from October 1 to March 31. Fishing is permitted at any time. Bicycles are allowed on designated trails and service roads.

Contact Info: Department of Conservation, 2360 Hwy. D, St. Charles, MO 63304. (636) 441-4554. www.conservation.state.mo.us.

Terrain: Mostly flat.

Rating: Moderate.

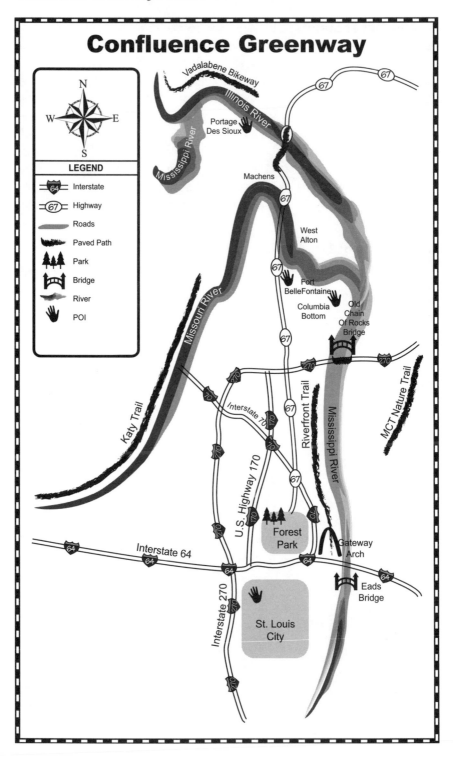

Confluence Greenway

LEGEND

- Interstate
- Highway
- Roads
- Paved Path
- Park
- Bridge
- River
- POI

Vadalabene Bikeway

Illinois River

Portage Des Sioux

Mississippi River

Machens

West Alton

Fort BelleFontaine

Columbia Bottom

Old Chain Of Rocks Bridge

Missouri River

Katy Trail

Interstate 70

Riverfront Trail

Mississippi River

MCT Nature Trail

U.S. Highway 170

Forest Park

Gateway Arch

Interstate 64

Interstate 270

St. Louis City

Eads Bridge

Confluence Greenway Project

Imagine, an 80-mile park spanning the shores of the Mississippi River with trails and beautiful scenic views of the river. This will be a reality. The Confluence Greenway project, when completed, will consist of a 40-mile riverside park on both sides of the Mississippi River, extending from the Gateway Arch in St. Louis, past the confluence of the Missouri River, to the confluence of the Mississippi and Illinois Rivers in Grafton, Illinois. Six nonprofit groups have teamed up to advance this project. The Greenway is expected to be completed by 2004, the bicentennial of the Lewis and Clark journey which began on land that will be part of the Confluence Greenway.

Key demonstration projects that are a part of the Confluence include:

Old Chain of Rocks Bridge

Completion of renovations, including structural work, connecting feeder trails amenities and river environment displays of this historic bridge. The Old Chain of Rocks Bridge is the second longest pedestrian/bicycle bridge in the world, and the longest pedestrian/bicycle river crossing. Open daily, one-half hour before sunrise to one-half hour after sunset.

Riverfront Trail

Bicycle patrols, prairie restoration, neighborhood involvement programs and maintenance of this new trail from the Gateway Arch to the Old Chain of Rocks Bridge.

Riverfront Heritage Trail Connection

Complete the trail from downtown East St. Louis to the river front including ecological enhancements such as native plantings and interpretative signs.

For more information about the Confluence Greenway project, please contact: The Confluence Greenway Project, 2100 Locust, Suite 2N, St. Louis, Missouri 63103. (314) 436-1324. Web site: www.confluencegreenway.org

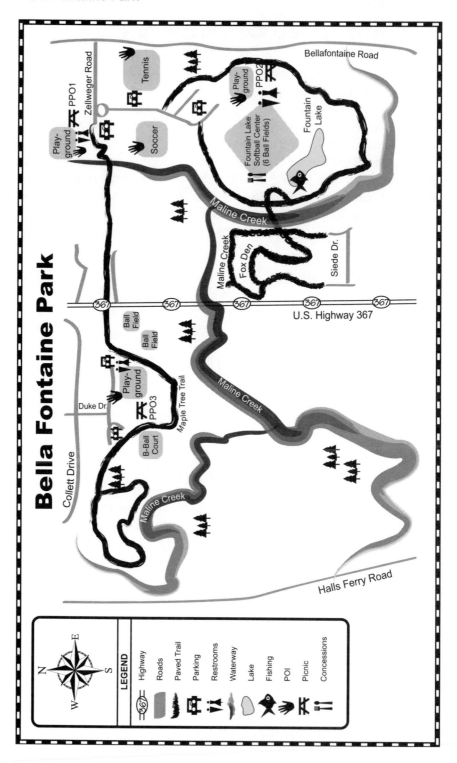

Bella Fontaine Park

Starting Point: Bellefontaine Neighbors, Missouri.

Directions to Starting Point: From North County take Interstate 270 to the Bellefontaine Road exit, go south. Go 1.8 miles and turn right onto Zellweger Road. Drive into the park on your left.

Approximate Pedaling Time: 30 minutes to one hour.

Distance: 3.1 miles of paved trails. Maple Tree Trail 1.0 miles, Cardinal Trail 1.3 miles, Maline Creek Trail 0.5 miles, Fox Den Trail 0.3 miles.

Ride Description: Paved multi-use trails through Bella Fontaine Park. The trails pass a small lake and travel along Maline Creek.

Things to See: Maline Creek and the park lake attract geese and other birds. The trails travel through wooded areas. The two-acre lake is open to fishermen of all ages.

Hazards: During softball season this place is busy with games.

Additional Thoughts: This is a fun trail to ride—a good place for a ride with kids. The trail crosses the creek on a curved bridge. There is a big softball complex here with six fields, scoreboard and bleachers.

Contact Info: St. Louis County Parks, 41 S. Central Ave., Clayton, MO 63105. (314) 615-7275 (PARK).

Terrain: Paved trail with some small hills.

Rating: Easy.

Notes:

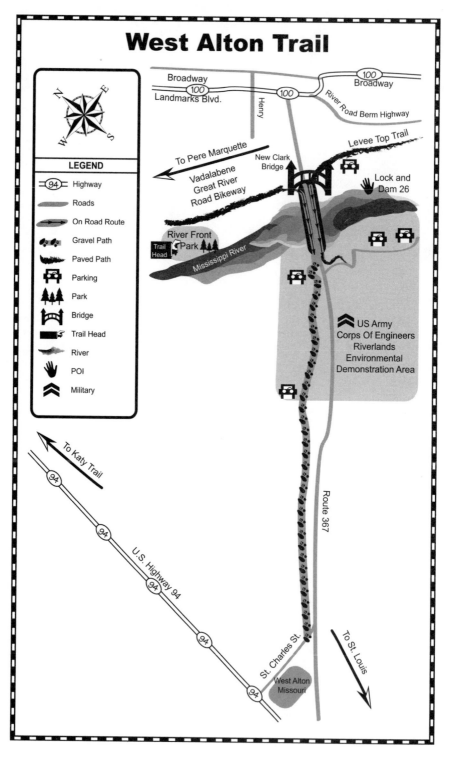

West Alton Trail

LEGEND

- ◯94◯ Highway
- Roads
- On Road Route
- Gravel Path
- Paved Path
- Parking
- Park
- Bridge
- Trail Head
- River
- POI
- Military

Broadway
100
Landmarks Blvd.

Henry

100

100
Broadway

River Road Berm Highway

To Pere Marquette

Vadalabene
Great River
Road Bikeway

New Clark
Bridge

Levee Top Trail

Lock and
Dam 26

River Front
Park

Trail
Head

Mississippi River

US Army
Corps Of Engineers
Riverlands
Environmental
Demonstration Area

To Katy Trail

94

94

U.S. Highway 94

94

94

Route 367

94

St. Charles St.

To St. Louis

West Alton
Missouri

Some day soon this scenic trail will be a key link between the Katy Trail and Illinois trails such as the Vadalabene Great River Road Bikeway.

West Alton Trail Bikeway & The Clark Bridge

Starting Point: River Front Park, Alton, Illinois.

Directions to Starting Point: Take Route 367 North, cross the Clark Bridge into Illinois. At light turn left onto Hwy. 100. Turn left on Henry (its just a little ways from the stoplight). Stay to the right and go into River Front Park. The park is by the Alton Belle Casino.

Approximate Pedaling Time: 1-2 hours.

Distance: 6 miles. (3 miles out, 3 miles back).

Ride Description: Paved and gravel bike paths with bridge crossing in bike lanes. From the parking lot follow the paved trail to the Clark Bridge. Cross the Clark Bridge using the designated bicycle lanes. Use caution as it can get very windy on the bridge and there is vehicle traffic. After crossing the bridge, the trail curves and continues on along the Riverlands Environmental Demonstration Area on a flat crushed limestone surfaced trail. This trail was formed from an old railroad bed. The trail extends to St. Charles Street in West Alton, Missouri. Turn around there and return the same way. If you don't wish to ride across the Clark Bridge you can park on the Missouri side at the Riverlands parking area.

Things to See: The trail runs alongside wetland areas with great opportunities for viewing birds, such as wintering Bald Eagles. Great Blue Herons and Egrets are other common sites. Woodchucks can be seen along the gravel trail. It's always fun to watch the Mississippi River roll by. In this area there is usually a lot of boat traffic.

Hazards: This is a gravel trail so be careful not to take a spill. The trail along the wetlands can get overgrown with vines at times. Use caution when crossing the Clark Bridge.

Additional Thoughts: A bicycle makes a great vehicle for exploring the gravel roads in the Riverlands Environmental Demonstration Area. Take along your binoculars for bird watching and exploring the native prairie restoration areas. Stop in at the Rivers Project Visitors Center. Some day this scenic trail will be a key link between the Katy Trail and Illinois trails such as the Vadalabene Great River Road Bikeway.

Contact Info: Trailnet Inc., 3900 Reavis Barracks, St. Louis, MO 63125. (314) 416-9930 or (618) 874-8554. Trailnet@trailnet.org. www.trailnet.org. Rivers Project Interpretive Center, 301 Riverlands Way, West Alton, MO 63386. (636) 899-2600 or (888) 899-2602.

Terrain: Flat, crushed limestone bike path.

Rating: Moderate.

Notes:

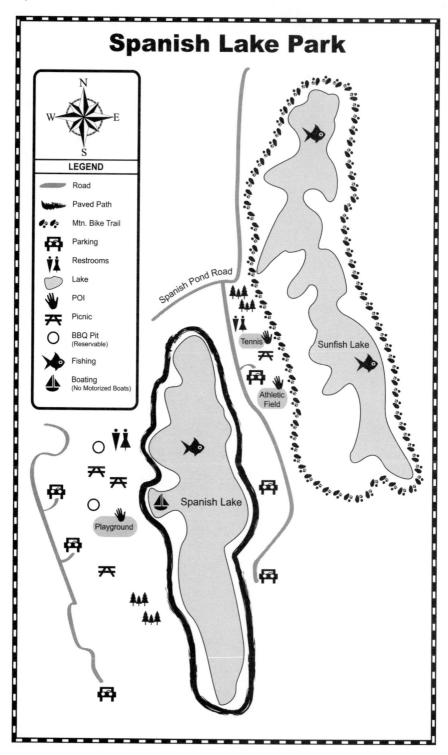

Spanish Lake Park
Paved Trail & Mountain Bike Trail

Starting Point: North St. Louis County, Missouri.

Directions to Starting Point: Take Interstate 270 north to the Bellefontaine Rd. exit. Turn left (north) on Bellefontaine Road. Turn right on Spanish Pond Road. There are three entrances to the park. The paved bicycle trail is located at the first entrance. The Mountain bike trails are located at the third entrance.

Spanish Lake Paved Trail

Approximate Pedaling Time: 10 minutes per lap.

Distance: Paved 1.4-mile loop.

Ride Description: Bicyclists, walkers, runners and rollerbladers share this paved path. It is a very scenic ride around Spanish Lake. This is a good place to take the kids.

Hazards: At times after heavy rains the lake can rise over the trail in sections. Mud on the trail can be very slick.

Sunfish Lake Mountain Bike Trail

Approximate Pedaling Time: 10-20 minutes per lap.

Distance: Dirt 1.2-mile loop trail.

Ride Description: Bicyclists, walkers, runners and hikers share this dirt trail. It's a very scenic ride around Sunfish Lake that goes through the woods and through grass fields along the lake's shores. Although this is a short trail, it makes for one of the best trails in the area to go to when looking for something fairly easy to ride on a mountain bike—even good for kids who are comfortable riding on dirt trails.

Hazards: The trail is poorly marked. Take insect repellent for the typical outdoor pests.

Things to See: Early last century, the area was called Spanish Pond. The park opened in 1971. This is a very pretty park. A large mature tree forest casts reflections into Spanish Lake. Geese and other wildlife like to visit the lake.

Additional Thoughts: There are many picnic tables and Bar-B-Q pits located in the park. Fishing is allowed in the lakes with a Missouri fishing license. Boats without gas motors may be used. There is a small boat dock on Spanish Lake and boat ramps on both lakes. Restrooms and drinking water are available.

Contact Info: St. Louis County Parks, 41 S. Central Ave., Clayton, MO 63105. (314) 615-7275 (PARK).

Terrain: Some small hills.

Rating: Easy.

The Spanish Lake Mountain Bike Trail
is a 1.2-mile loop around Sunfish Lake.

Notes:

ILLINOIS

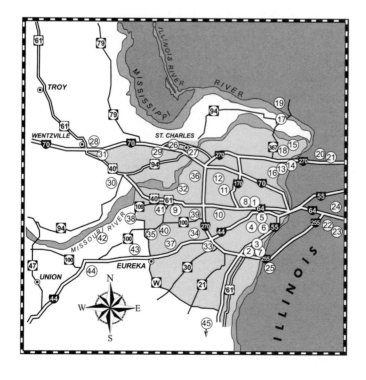

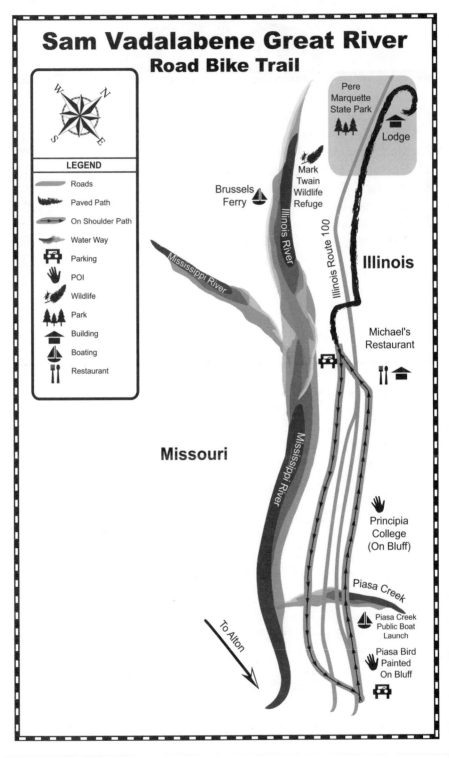

Sam Vadalabene Great River
Road Bike Trail

LEGEND

- Roads
- Paved Path
- On Shoulder Path
- Water Way
- Parking
- POI
- Wildlife
- Park
- Building
- Boating
- Restaurant

Pere Marquette State Park

Lodge

Mark Twain Wildlife Refuge

Brussels Ferry

Illinois River

Illinois Route 100

Illinois

Michael's Restaurant

Missouri

Mississippi River

Mississippi River

Principia College (On Bluff)

Piasa Creek

Piasa Creek Public Boat Launch

Piasa Bird Painted On Bluff

To Alton

Sam Vadalabene
Great River Road Bike Trail

Starting Point: Great River Road (Illinois Route 100) Alton, Illinois, at bicycle parking area.

Directions to Starting Point: Take Interstate 270 to Hwy. 367 North to Alton. After crossing the Clark Bridge, turn left on Illinois Route 100 (the Great River Road). Go through Alton and look for the bicycle parking area on the right side with the Piasa bird painted on the bluff.

Approximate Pedaling Time: 2.5-5 hours. Ride can be cut short at any of the openings in the medians.

Distance: 41.4 miles round trip (20.7 miles each way) if ridden the entire distance from Alton to Pere Marquette State Park, then back to Alton. The trip can be shortened at any breaks in the median. It is recommended to dismount and walk your bike across the highway.

Ride Description: This popular, flat, paved, bike trail stretches from Alton to Pere Marquette State Park on the Illinois side of the Mississippi River. Most of this trail is on a bike path separate from vehicle traffic. There is a section several miles long east of Grafton

Michael's Restaurant

that the trail becomes on-road bicycle lanes. In Grafton the bike trail turns towards the river (follow signs) and travels on a paved path that is between the river and Hwy. 100 (the Great River Rd.). After Grafton, the paved path crosses Hwy. 100 (the Great River Road) and continues on between the road and the bluffs. There are a few hills near the Brussels Ferry.

Things to See: Great views of the Mississippi River and Bluffs. Eagles nest along the bluffs and can be seen fishing in the river between December 1st and March 1st. The river towns of Alton, Elsah and Grafton have great food and good antique shopping. Michael's restaurant in Grafton has good food and memorable pies.

Hazards: Road hazards, traffic, holes and debris. It can get windy at times. Use caution when crossing the road.

Additional Thoughts: Riding the entire 41.4-mile route makes for a great all day adventure. It can get very busy in nice weather, and at times can get very windy. When traveling on bike trails located on the shoulder of the highway, travel in the direction of traffic only. Bikes are subject to the same rules as motor vehicles. The sections with the separate bike path are nice to take the kids on.

Contact Info: Illinois Department of Natural Resources, 524 S. Second Street, Springfield, IL 62701-1787. (217) 782-7454. Trailnet, Inc., 3900 Reavis Barracks, St. Louis, MO 63125. (314) 416-9930 or (618) 874-8554. E-mail: trailnet@trailnet.org. Website: www.trailnet.org.

Terrain: Flat paved bikeway with a few hills near Brussels Ferry. There is a bikeway on a separate bike path and bike path lanes on the roadway.

Rating: Moderately difficult.

Be sure to play a game with the life-size chess pieces at Pere Marquette State Park Lodge along the Illinois Great River Road.

Recreated Piasa bird painting on bluff near Alton, Illinois, along the Great River Road Bike Route.

....Just as the beast was about to sink its huge talons into the chief, the warriors all shot the poisoned arrows. The arrows struck the beast and with a fierce chilling scream of pain, the beast died. Chief Ouatoga and his warriors and tribes were saved....

Piasa Legend

The bird-like monster, known as the Piasa, lived along the bluffs of the Mighty Mississippi River long before any European explorers reached the banks here. The birdlike creature would swoop down from the bluff and grasp its prey in its massive talons. The creature could carry off a large deer, but preferred human flesh. Indian warriors attempted to kill the beast but failed. The Piasa bird wiped out many villages in this area.

The great Chief Ouatoga fasted for one whole moon and prayed to the Great Spirit to save his people from the beast. In a dream, the Great Spirit directed Ouatoga to gather twenty of his bravest warriors and arm them with bows and poisoned arrows and have another warrior draw the beast out into the open by standing in a field near the bluffs. The chief told his tribe of his dream. The warriors were selected and the ambush of the Piasa beast was planned.

The Great Chief Ouatoga offered himself as the victim to lure the beast into the awaiting ambush. Standing atop the bluff the Piasa beast soon spotted the Chief in the field. As the beast swooped down the Chief chanted the death song of the warrior. Just as the beast was about to sink its huge talons into the chief, the warriors all shot the poisoned arrows. The arrows struck the beast, and with a fierce chilling scream of pain, the beast died. Chief Ouatoga and his warriors and tribes were saved.

When the first European explorers traveled through this area they saw the giant birdlike beast carved high up in the bluffs towering over the Mississippi River. Just how the giant carving got there and its original placement along the river is still a mystery.

In 1998, the Piasa bird was restored using the written description found in Pere Marquette's journals.

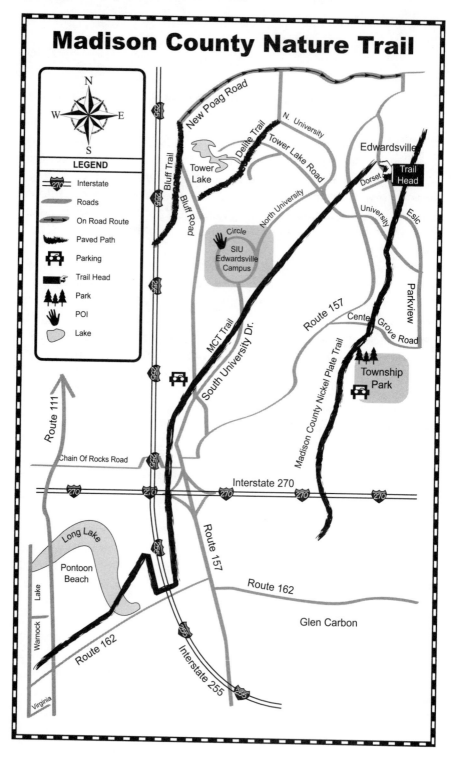

Madison County Nature Trail

LEGEND

Interstate
Roads
On Road Route
Paved Path
Parking
Trail Head
Park
POI
Lake

New Poag Road
N. University
Deltie Trail
Tower Lake Road
Edwardsville
Bluff Trail
Tower Lake
Dorset
Trail Head
Bluff Road
North University
University
Esic
Circle
SIU Edwardsville Campus
MCT Trail
South University Dr.
Route 157
Center Grove Road
Parkview
Madison County Nickel Plate Trail
Township Park
Route 111
Chain Of Rocks Road
Interstate 270
Long Lake
Route 157
Pontoon Beach
Route 162
Lake
Glen Carbon
Warnock
Route 162
Interstate 255
Virginia

Look for the big barn on Bluff Road at Edwardsville, Illinois. The barn is across the road from the parking lot and trailhead for the Vadalabene Nature Trail.

Madison County
Transit Nature Trail

Starting Point: Edwardsville, Illinois.

Directions to Starting Point: From St. Louis take Interstate 270 northeast into Illinois. Exit Hwy. 157 north. Turn right on Center Grove Road. Turn left on Esic Drive. Drive 0.8 mile, the trail will be on the left. Parking is allowed along one side of the road. If it's too congested you may park at Township Park at the intersection of Center Grove Road and Esic.

Approximate Pedaling Time: 2 hours.

Distance: 20.2 miles round trip. (10.1 miles out, 10.1 miles back).

Ride Description: This is a paved bike/multi-use path (SIU-Edwardsville to Warnock Lake Road). The trail starts at Esic Road and travels southwest through SIU's campus, over Interstate 270 and under Interstate 255. Other trails in the area include the Madison County Nickel Plate Trail, Bluff Trail, Delite W. Morris Trail and the Glen Carbon Heritage Trail. (See next section.)

Things to See: This is a wonderful path and great for kids. The path travels along a creek for a few miles then cuts across flat farmland. The small wetlands along the trail are home to many small creatures. The spring chorus of frogs is a joy to hear. Many birds and wildflowers also enjoy the greenway.

Hazards: Use caution at road crossings. At one point after the crossing over I-270 there is a split in the trail that leads to an overlook.

Additional Thoughts: This is one of the best bike paths in the area. Food and bike shops are available in Edwardsville. At this time there are no restrooms or drinking water along the trail. This trail also connects to the SIU trails around the university and the Delyte Morris Bikeway that extends another 2.3 miles to New Poag / St. Louis Road.

Contact Info: Madison County Transit (618) 874-7433. Fax (618) 797-7547.

Terrain: Mostly flat.

Trail Status: Madison County Transit. (618) 874-7443.

Rating: Moderate.

From the Vadalabene Nature Trail, you can take the Delyte Morris Bikeway to connect with SIU-Edwardsville.

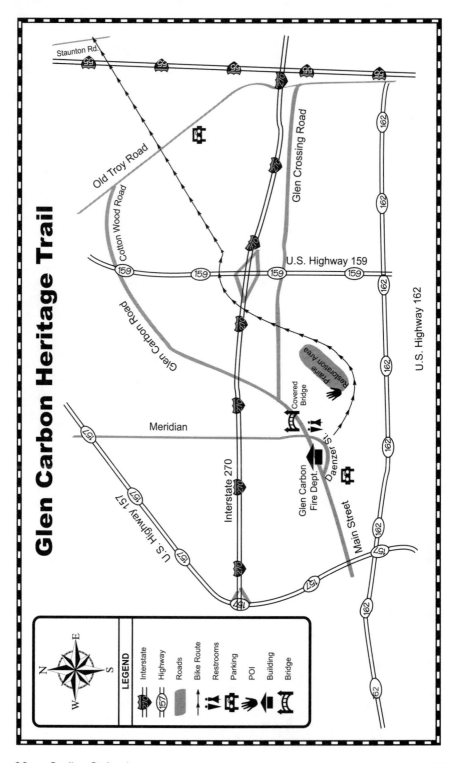

Ronald J. Foster
Glen Carbon Heritage Trail

Starting Point: Glen Carbon, Illinois.

Directions to Starting Point: Take Interstate 270 to Illinois Route 157 South .8 mile. Then turn right on Glen Carbon Road (Main Street). Travel 1 mile, go across the railroad tracks and turn right after the Fire Department (Daenzer Ave.). Follow parking signs to the right, behind building to the trailhead.

Approximate Pedaling Time: 2-4 hours with stops to read information kiosks.

Distance: 13.4 miles round-trip. (6.7 miles out, 6.7 miles back).

Ride Description: Flat rail-to-trail conversion with bridges.

Things to See: The prairie restoration area is worth checking out. You might see rabbits, squirrels, larger wildlife and a variety of birds. Be sure and read the information kiosks on the corridor's history. You may see some interesting birds on the many birdhouses along the trail and at one point old telephone poles with glass insulators.

Hazards: This trail is asphalt with gravel on top. The gravel can be tricky on steering. Use caution at road crossings.

Additional Thoughts: Great to take the kids. Take a short ride on-road on Glen Carbon's bike route across the covered bridge to Miner Park. More history kiosks are there plus playgrounds, picnic areas and pavilion. Restrooms and drinking water are available here. Drinking water facilities are also available at the Mont Station Rest Area. Parking at west trail head is behind the fire station. Additional parking is available at Mount Station where the trail crosses Old Troy Road and at Khun Station. Trail maps are available at all parking areas and at each road crossing.

Contact Info: Village of Glen Carbon, P.O. Box 757, R151 North Main, Glen Carbon, IL 62034-0757. (618) 288-1200.

Terrain: Flat rail-to-trail conversion. Asphalt with brown gravel.

Rating: Easy.

The Glen Carbon covered bridge signals your arrival to town.

The Glen Carbon Trail usually takes two hours to ride. Give yourself
at least three to four if you plan on reading the very informative kiosks.

The above sign says it all.

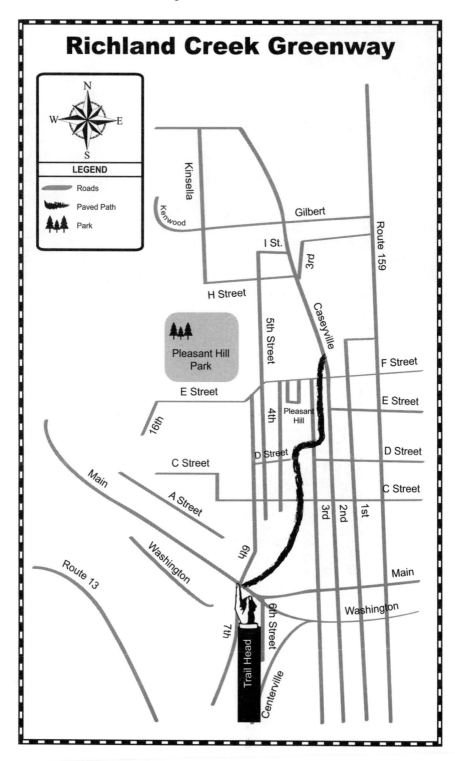

Richland Creek Greenway

Richland Creek Greenway

Starting Point: Rotary Park, Belleville, Illinois.

Directions to Starting Point: From St. Louis take Interstate 270 southeast. It turns into I-255 to Illinois. Take it north to Hwy. 15 South. From 15, turn left onto Centerville. Turn left on Main Street, turn right on 6th Street North, the park is on the right.

Approximate Pedaling Time: 10 minutes.

Distance: 1.2 miles round trip. (0.6 miles out, 0.6 miles back).

Ride Description: Flat multi-use trail with small on-road section. The trail travels from the park, through a small greenway area and ends after crossing Richland Creek at 2nd Street.

Things to See: Richland Creek and several large metal sculptures.

Hazards: Use caution at road crossings. There are some on-road sections off this trail. Watch for traffic, holes, gravel, and road hazards.

Additional Thoughts: This is the trail that didn't happen. The project was designed to be a 6-mile trail along Richland Creek that was never completed by the City of Belleville. It's not worth the trip to just ride this trail, but could be used if out exploring the city of Belleville.

Contact Info: City of Belleville.

Terrain: Flat.

Rating: Easy.

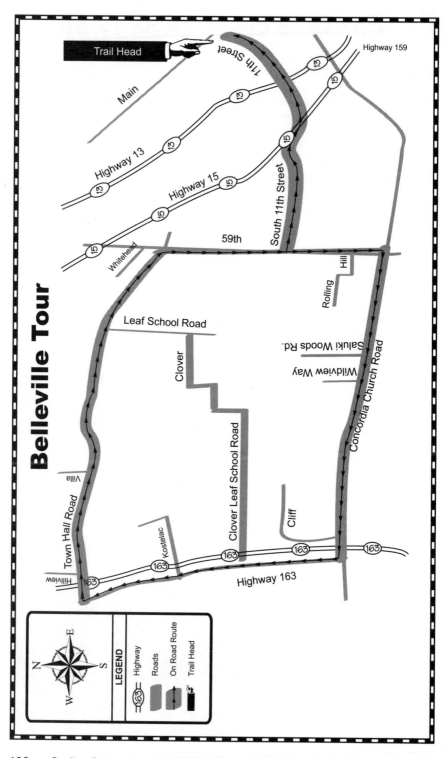

Photo by Peggy Welch.

Belleville Tour

Starting Point: Belleville, Illinois.

Directions to Starting Point: From St. Louis take Interstate 270 southeast. It turns into I-255 to Illinois. Take it north to Hwy. 15 South. From 15, turn left onto Hwy. 13. Turn right onto 11th Street and follow to Main Street. Turn left on Main and park.

Approximate Pedaling Time: 1-2 hours.

Distance: 15 miles.

Ride Description: On-road route with rolling hills. From Main Street go south on 11th Street. Cycle 2.5 miles. Turn LEFT on South 59th 0.8 miles to Concordia Church Road. Turn RIGHT on Concordia Church Road. Cycle 2.6 miles to IL Route 163. Turn RIGHT on 163 Cycle 2.1 miles. Turn RIGHT on Town Hall Road. Cycle 3.8 miles. Turn RIGHT on South 59th. Cycle 0.8 miles. Turn LEFT on 11th Street. Cycle 2.5 miles back to the starting point.

Things to See: Farmland around Belleville and historic old buildings.

Hazards: Caution at road crossings. Holes and gravel.

Additional Thoughts: Not recommended for kids. For bicycling needs or other possible bike routes in Belleville check out Endres Schwinn Cycling & Fitness at 3625 W. Main St. (618) 233-0378 or Bicycle World Inc. at 4516 W. Main St. (618) 234-0041.

Terrain: Rolling hills.   **Rating:** Moderately difficult.

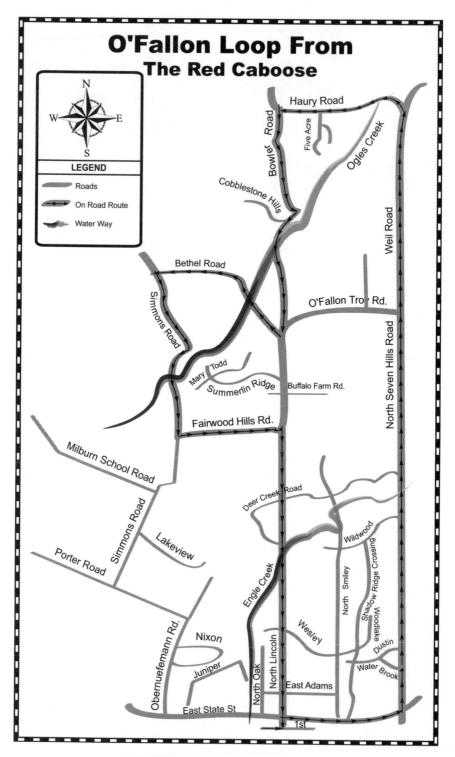

O'Fallon Loop From
The Red Caboose

Preparing for a ride in the Red Caboose parking lot in downtown O'Fallon.
Photo by Cynthia Thompson.

O'Fallon Loop from the Red Caboose

Starting Point: O'Fallon, Illinois.

Directions to Starting Point: From St. Louis take Interstate 64 east to the O'Fallon exit. Turn left and follow Hwy. 50. Turn left onto State Street just before the Convenient Food Mart gas station. Turn Right on South Lincoln, cross railroad tracks, turn right onto West 1st Street and into the parking lot with the Red Caboose.

Approximate Pedaling Time: 1-1.5 hours.

Distance: 13 miles.

Ride Description: From the Red Caboose parking lot at First Street and Lincoln, cycle north on Lincoln just over the railroad tracks turn RIGHT on East State Street. LEFT on North Seven Hills Road, just past the water tower. Watch for chickens in a yard at the top of one of the hills. At Stop sign (4 miles) continue straight, name of road changes to Weil Road. At about the 5.2 mile mark turn LEFT on Haury Road, it goes downhill. At about the 6.4 mile mark the road makes a sharp curve, before the curve make a LEFT turn onto Bowler

Road. This is a pretty wooded area. Continue on to Stop sign (7.9 miles), go a little ways and turn RIGHT on Bethel School Road. Watch for elk on the right side of the road at about the 9-mile mark. At the sharp curve turn LEFT onto Simmons Road. Turn LEFT on Fairwood Hills Road (13.4 miles). Turn RIGHT onto Lincoln for about 1 mile to 1st Street and the Red Caboose parking lot.

Things to See: Stop in at the O'Fallon Historical Society, located at the corner of West State and Lincoln. They have a great collection of local artifacts. Brian and Doris, the local historians, are full of area knowledge. The Red Caboose has a display inside on area railroad history. It's open on special occasions. The Bicycle Zone bicycle shop, on the northwest corner of State and Lincoln, is housed in one of the oldest buildings in O'Fallon, built in 1855. Simmons Road is a very scenic road that travels along Ogles Creek.

Hazards: Watch for on-road hazards, holes, cracks, loose gravel and traffic. Lincoln and Kyle Roads can get busy.

Additional Thoughts: Visit Stewart and Missy Drolet at the Bicycle Zone bicycle shop. They are at the corner of State Street and Lincoln Streets.

Terrain: Moderate with some hills.

Rating: Moderately difficult.

The Historical Society in O'Fallon, Illinois,
is worth a visit to extend your daytrip explorations.

American Youth Hostels (AYH) Gateway Council Hostelling International

Most people know about hostelling from trips to Europe during their college years, getting a Euro pass and staying in unique hotel-like facilities. Locally though, the Gateway Council of the AYH is involved in much more than just hostels. They provide organized bicycle rides almost weekly, plus an entire calendar of adventure rides. Through the efforts of the many dedicated volunteers, the AYH events offer marked routes, food on several, a "sag-wagon" service and a monthly newspaper. Some of their most enjoyable events include:

C.A.M.P.

A weeklong ride to Missouri state parks. Each night the "CAMPers" stay in a different park. The ride is supported with a "sag-wagon" and breakfast and dinner is provided each day. This trip makes for a wonderful bicycling vacation.

Moonlight Ramble

This is the country's largest nighttime ride, with as many as 22,000 riders participating. The ride starts at midnight. Riders cruise a 15 to 20 mile course through the streets of downtown St. Louis. It's quite a sight to see—a party on wheels.

Natalie G. Kekeisen Flat as a Pancake Century

This ride is named in honor of Natalie who was a well-known and well-liked cyclist and volunteer for the AYH. This event follows a 100-mile course through the flat roads of Illinois.

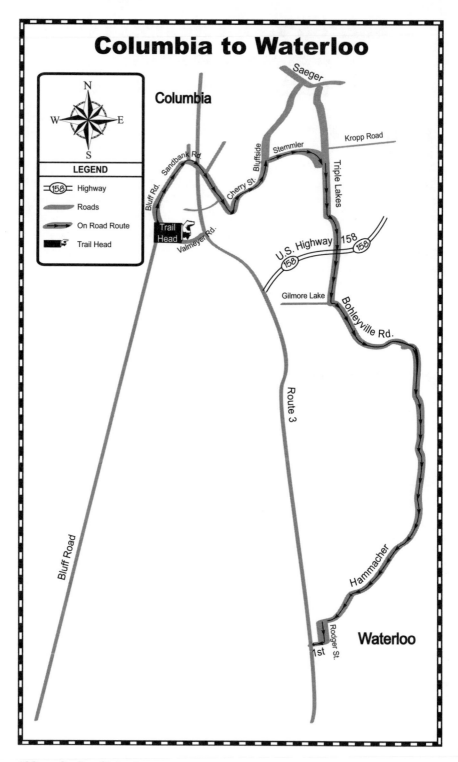

Columbia to Waterloo

Columbia

LEGEND

- 158 Highway
- Roads
- On Road Route
- Trail Head

Saeger

Kropp Road

Stemmler

Bluffside

Cherry St.

Sandbank Rd.

Bluff Rd.

Triple Lakes

Trail Head

Valmeyer Rd.

U.S. Highway 158

158   158

Gilmore Lake

Bohleyville Rd.

Route 3

Bluff Road

Hammacher

Rodger St.

Waterloo

1st

Columbia to Waterloo

Starting Point: Market Place, Columbia, Illinois.

Directions to Starting Point: Interstate 255 to the Columbia, Illinois Route 3 exit. Continue into town, the Market Place is behind McDonalds at 1000 Columbia Centre.

Approximate Pedaling Time: 2.5-3.5 hours.

Distance: 35 miles.

Ride Description: Cycle south of Market Place to Valmeyer Road. Turn RIGHT onto Valmeyer. Stay to the right of the fork in the road. RIGHT on Bluff Road. RIGHT on Sand Bank, cross Rt. 3. The road becomes Main Street. LEFT on Cherry Street up big hill (nicknamed cemetery hill because of the cemetery on the left). By the cemetery take the LEFT fork, which is Bluffside. Continue on Bluffside to Stemmler. RIGHT on Stemmler. RIGHT on Triple Lakes. Left on Bohleyville Road. RIGHT on Hammacher (Bohleyville Road). LEFT on Roger Street. Right on 1st Street and welcome to Waterloo. The Lincoln Trail Restaurant, at 1st and Market Streets, has good food. Riders who do this ride often stop there. Return the same way.

Things to See: Very scenic ride through Illinois farm country. Lincoln Trail Restaurant in Waterloo is a good place to stop and eat.

Hazards: Road hazards, holes, cracks, gravel, traffic.

Additional Thoughts: The Market Place is a grocery store. This area is very popular with cyclists. This route is one of the AYH's Tuesday rides.

Terrain: Moderately hilly.

Rating: Difficult.

ST. CHARLES COUNTY

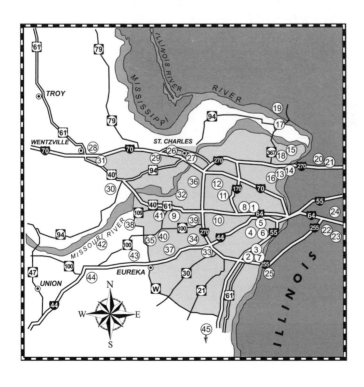

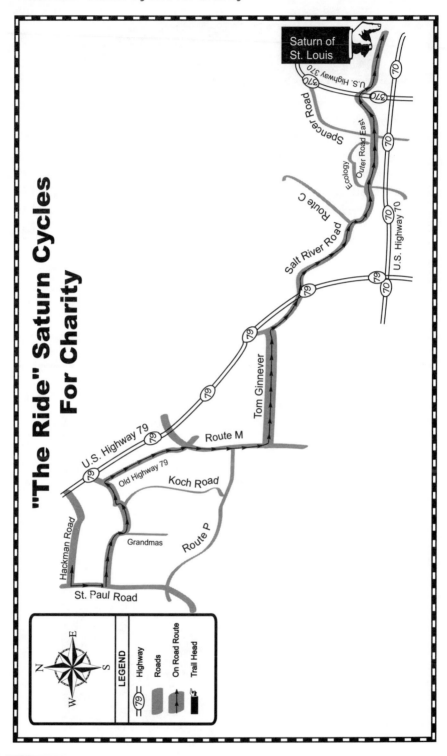

"The Ride"
Saturn Cycles for Charity

Through a commitment to community involvement by the Lou Fusz Automotive Network and the Saturn Corporation "The Ride" was created. Although the event hasn't been held for several years, it is still a challenging and scenic ride for street cyclists.

"The Ride" – Saturn Cycles for Charity

Starting Point: Saturn of St. Charles, St. Charles County, Missouri.

Directions to Starting Point: From St. Louis take Interstate 70 west. Take the Cave Springs exit. Turn right, then left onto the North Service Road west. Saturn of St. Charles will be on the right.

Approximate Pedaling Time: 2.5 hours.

Distance: 25 miles.

Ride Description: On-road bicycle route. From the parking lot of Saturn of St. Charles, Turn RIGHT on the north service road. Past Mid Rivers Mall Drive, the name of the road changes to Main St.

Follow Main St. through Old Town St. Peters. Turn LEFT on Salt River Road. Turn RIGHT on Pearl. Turn LEFT on Tom Ginnever Ave. Turn RIGHT on Hwy. M. Turn LEFT on Old Hwy. 79. Be careful as this turn is easy to miss. (If you get to Hwy. 79 turn back one block). Turn LEFT on Mueller Road. Turn RIGHT on St. Paul Road. Turn RIGHT on Hackman Road. Go one block to the fire station. This is the turnaround point.

Things to See: Old town St. Peters.

Hazards: Road hazards such as traffic, holes, debris on road.

Additional Thoughts: Saturn of St. Louis has not organized this ride for the last few years, but they have not ruled out the possibility of future rides.

Terrain: Some hills.

Rating: Moderate.

"The Ride" – Saturn Cycles for Charity.

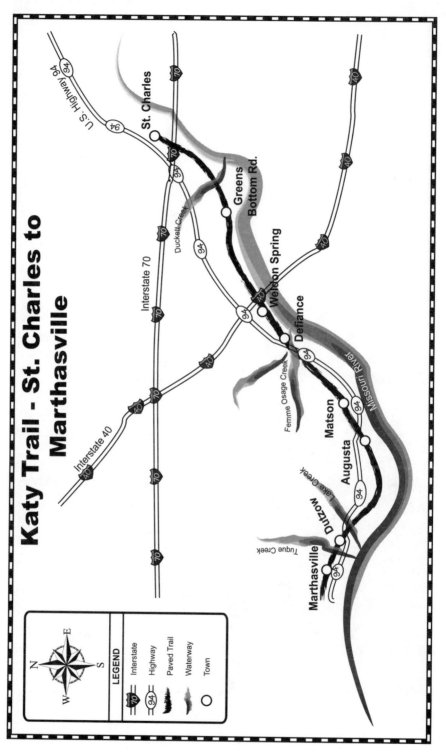

Katy Trail - St. Charles to Marthasville

LEGEND

Interstate
Highway
Paved Trail
Waterway
Town

Katy Trail State Park
St. Charles to Marthasville

Starting Point: Frontier Park, St. Charles, Missouri.

Directions to Starting Point: From St. Louis take Interstate 70 west to South Fifth Street Exit. Turn right on South Fifth to Boonslick Road, turn right. Boonslick Road will take you to Riverside. There are several parking areas along Riverside near Frontier Park.

Approximate Pedaling Time: One hour up to four hours one way, or eight hours for the entire trip out to Marthasville and back.

Distance: 38.2 miles one way. You can turn around at any point on the trail.

Ride Description: Multi-use trail with hard pack chat surface. The Katy Trail is the country's longest rail-to-trail conversion. For the trip to Marthasville these trailhead services are available:

St. Charles - Mile marker 39.5: All services are available here including bike shop, lodging, restaurants, restrooms and water.

Greens Bottom Road - Mile marker 45.7: Restrooms and parking.

Weldon Spring - Mile marker 56: Restrooms and parking.

Defiance - Mile marker 59.1: Bicycle rental, lodging, food, restrooms, drinking water and parking.

Matson - Mile marker 60.6: Restrooms and parking.

Augusta - Mile marker 66.3: Bike shop, bike rental, lodging, food, restrooms, drinking water and parking.

Dutzow - Mile marker 74: Bike rental, lodging, food, restrooms, drinking water and parking.

Marthasville - Mile marker 77.7: Bike shop, bike rental, lodging, food, restrooms, drinking water and parking.

Things to See: The Katy Trail provides adventures for everyone. St. Charles was the First Capital of Missouri. Check out the Lewis and Clark museum and the many shops along Main Street in St. Charles. This area, considered to be the Rhineland of Missouri, attracted many German settlers. The small towns along the trail are fun to explore.

Hazards: Use caution at road crossings. The edges of the trail tend to be soft. Yes, you should wear your helmet here, too! Occasional wildlife on the trail.

Additional Thoughts: The trail is marked every mile. Great place for kids. The trail is only open during daylight hours. Scenic Cycles and the Touring Cyclist provide shuttle services. For more information on the Katy Trail order The Complete Katy Trail Guidebook ($16.95) from Pebble Publishing, Inc. (800) 576-7322. Or go online at www.pebblepublishing.com.

Contact Info: Missouri Department of Natural Resources: (800) 361-4827. Website: www.dnr.state.mo.us. Scenic Cycles Marthasville: (636) 433-2909. E-mail: info@scenic-cycles.com. Website: www.scenic-cycles.com. Touring Cyclist, St. Charles: (636) 949-9630. E-mail: info@touringcyclist.com. Website: www.touringcyclist.com.

Terrain: Flat rails-to-trails conversion.

Trail Status: Department of Natural Resources.

Rating: Moderate.

Tom Yarbrough explaining the Fun Club's two word philosophy: Have fun.

The Trailnet Bicycle Fun Club

Way back in 1979 Tom Yarbrough began organizing bicycle rides in the St. Louis area for The Touring Cyclist. Several years later, Tom began his own bicycle business, the "Bicycle Fun Club," promoting bicycling in the area with more than 30 events a year. In 2000, the club affiliated with Trailnet.

The activities range from one-day rides of 15 miles to two-day adventures. The Club likes to ride quiet country roads to small towns where the stores, restaurants and taverns serve as rest stops. These rides are "supported" events, with a "sag-wagon" service van that cruises the route, giving out cold water, bananas and cookies. If you have a flat tire, the Fun Club's support crew can fix it for you and if you're just too tired to finish, they can give you a ride.

If you're a bit hesitant to get out and ride by yourself this is the answer. At each event the Fun Club distributes route maps to all participants and marks all turns directly on the roads. The Strawberry Festival ride in May has been the favorite ride over the years along with the weekly Wednesday and Thursday night rides. For a calendar of upcoming rides and other Fun Club information, check out their website at www.bicyclefunclub.org.

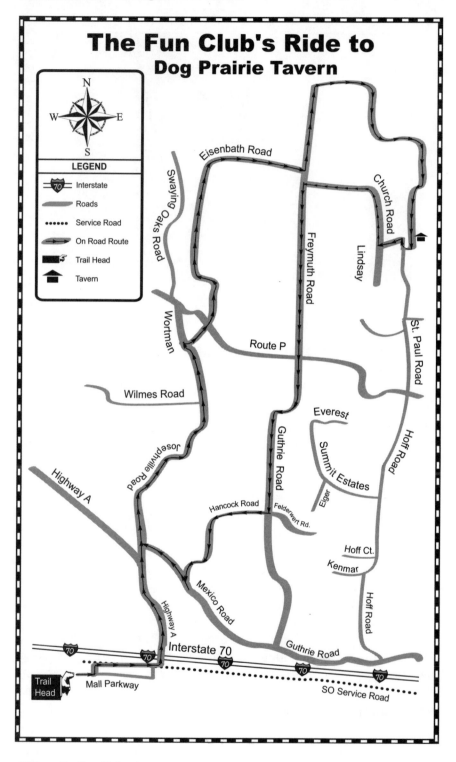

The Fun Club's Ride to
Dog Prairie Tavern

LEGEND

🛣️ Interstate

Roads

•••••• Service Road

On Road Route

Trail Head

Tavern

Eisenbath Road

Church Road

Swaying Oaks Road

Freymuth Road

Lindsay

Wortman

Route P

St. Paul Road

Wilmes Road

Everest

Josephville Road

Guthrie Road

Summit Estates

Hoff Road

Highway A

Eiger

Hancock Road

Felderwert Rd.

Hoff Ct.

Kenmar

Mexico Road

Highway A

Hoff Road

🛣️70

Interstate 70

Guthrie Road

🛣️70

🛣️70

🛣️70

🛣️70

Trail Head

Mall Parkway

SO Service Road

The Fun Club's Dog Prairie Tavern Ride is a popular scenic ride along the Cuiver River Valley area.

The Fun Club's Ride to Dog Prairie Tavern

Starting Point: Mall at Wentzville Crossing, Wentzville, Missouri.

Directions to Starting Point: From St. Louis take Interstate 70 west to exit 212 for Hwy. A. Turn left on A. Turn right on South Outer Road West to the Mall.

Approximate Pedaling Time: 2-3 hours.

Distance: 22 miles.

Ride Description: On-road route. Cycle from the Mall east on the South Outer road towards Lake St. Louis. Turn LEFT on Hwy. A and ride under Interstate 70. Turn RIGHT on Josephville Road. Josephville Road becomes Eisenbath after the town of Josephville, stay right. Turn LEFT on Freymuth. Turn RIGHT on Hwy. Y. Turn RIGHT at St. Paul Road. You'll see the Dog Prairie Tavern on the left. Turn RIGHT on Church. Turn LEFT on Freymuth which becomes Gutherie. Turn RIGHT on Hancock Road. RIGHT at Mexico Road. Mexico Road "T's" into Josephville Road, turn LEFT. At Hwy. A turn LEFT. Turn RIGHT on South Outer Road back to the Mall.

Things to See: This is a very popular scenic ride along the Cuiver River Valley area.

Hazards: Traffic, road hazards, holes, debris on road, dogs.

Additional Thoughts: This is one of the Fun Club's best rides.

Contact Info: Bicycle Fun Club, 3900 Reavis Barracks Road, St. Louis, Missouri 63125. 314-416-9930 or 618-874-8554. Website: www.bicyclefunclub.org.

Terrain: Somewhat Hilly.

Rating: Difficult.

Be mindful of the street signs in St. Paul. The streets can be a bit confusing here.

St. Paul's Catholic Church in St. Paul, Missouri—Photo by Cynthia Thompson

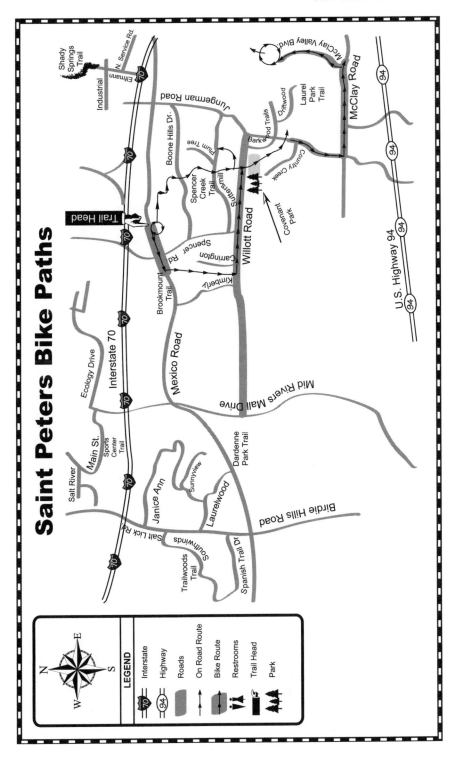

St. Peters Bike Paths

Starting Point: Recplex, St. Peters, Missouri.

Directions to Starting Point: From St. Louis take Interstate 70 west to the Cave Springs exit. Turn left on Cave Springs Road. Turn Right on Mexico Road. The Recplex and City Centre Park will be on the left. Trails start by the ballfields.

Approximate Pedaling Time: 1-1½ hours.

Distance: 10 miles.

Ride Description: On-Road and Bike Path. From City Center Park (Recplex) ride the trail that loops through the park then follow the Spencer Creek trail. This trail travels through several neighborhoods along the creek and connects City Center Park, Spencer Creek Park and Covenant Park. Where the trail intersects Jungermann Road turn RIGHT. Continue on Jungermann Road south to McClay Road, turn LEFT. Turn LEFT onto McClay Valley Blvd. Follow McClay Valley Blvd. into Laurel Park. Ride the loop trail at the park. Return to the Recplex the same way. Take McClay Valley Blvd. to McClay Road. Turn RIGHT on McClay Road. Turn LEFT on Jungermann Road. Turn LEFT on the Spencer Creek trail. Turn LEFT on Willott Road. Travel west on Willott Road 1.2 miles watch for the entrance of the

Brookmount Trail. Turn RIGHT on the Brookmount Trail. Follow the trail to Mexico Road, turn RIGHT. Take Mexico Road back to the Recplex and City Center Park.

Things to See: This trail travels along Spencer Creek and connects several neighborhoods and parks.

Hazards: Can get busy on weekends and nice days. Bicyclists, walkers, runners and rollerbladers share this trail.

Additional Thoughts: St. Peters has over 580 acres of parks, with almost 8 miles of paved trails. The Recplex is 124,000 square feet of family recreation and athletic training areas. Sports enjoyed there are swimming, ice skating, running, aerobics, dance, basketball, tennis, soccer and volleyball. The on-road parts of this ride follow some of St. Peters multi-use recreational trail. The City of St. Peters has some of the best parks in the area. Bike shops are close by on Mid Rivers Mall Drive. The trail sections of this ride are great for the kids, especially the loop trail in Laurel Park. This would be a fun ride to take along a picnic lunch.

Contact Info: City of St. Peters Recplex, 5200 Mexico Road, St. Peters, MO 63376. (636) 939-2386.

Terrain: Rolling hills.

Rating: Moderate.

Bridge along the Spencer Creek Trail is narrow. Be courteous to other trail users.
Photo by Walt Goodman.

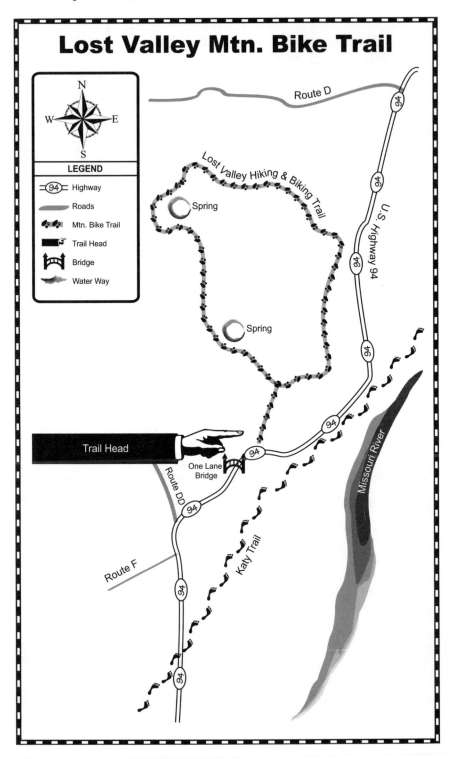

Lost Valley Mtn. Bike Trail

LEGEND

- 94 Highway
- Roads
- Mtn. Bike Trail
- Trail Head
- Bridge
- Water Way

Route D

94

U.S. Highway 94

Lost Valley Hiking & Biking Trail

Spring

Spring

94

94

Trail Head

One Lane Bridge

Route DD

94

Route F

94

94

94

Katy Trail

Missouri River

Lost Valley Mountain Bike Trail

Starting Point: Weldon Spring Conservation Area, St. Charles County.

Directions to Starting Point: From St. Louis take Interstate 64/40 west to Hwy. 94. Go south on Hwy. 94 for 6 miles to the gravel parking area on the right. The trailhead is marked with a sign.

Approximate Pedaling Time: 1-3 hours.

Distance: 8-mile loop.

Ride Description: Dirt multi-use trail shared by mountain bicyclists, hikers and hunters. This eight-mile loop is one of the best trails in the area for beginners who like challenges and intermediate riders. Most of the trail is wide and, except for two major hills, there is little climbing. The trail will take you along the Little Femme Osage Creek and past two spring-fed lakes. You'll cross a dry creek bed on a wooden bridge, then climb a good-sized hill. Towards the end of the ride watch for the right turn at the bottom of a large gravel downhill. It is easy to miss this turn and end up way off the trail. After making that turn you'll ride through a valley, cross through a creek and on to the last leg of single track. While on this single-track section be on the lookout for several varieties of ferns growing along the trail. A short climb then you'll be back on the main wide trail that leads back to the parking lot.

Things to See: The wildflowers are great in both spring and summer. During the spring some sections of the trail are engulfed with white and blue wildflowers. Blue Herons, kingfishers and indigo bunting are some of the birds you may see. This is a great place to take the wildflower and bird guidebooks along.

Hazards: Take a map and watch for the turn in the trail at the bottom of the large gravel downhill. Take the bug repellent and check yourself for ticks. Do not drink from the springs or creeks as they may be contaminated. Hunting is allowed. Call the Department of Conservation for information on hunting seasons.

Additional Thoughts: There is no water and no restrooms here.

Contact Info: Weldon Spring Conservation Area (636) 441-4554.

Terrain: Wide valley trails, some gravel road, a bit of single track.

Rating: Moderately difficult.

The Lost Valley Mountain Bike Trail meandors past the scenic Little Femme Osage Creek and two spring-fed lakes.

It's a good idea to slow down for bridge crossings.

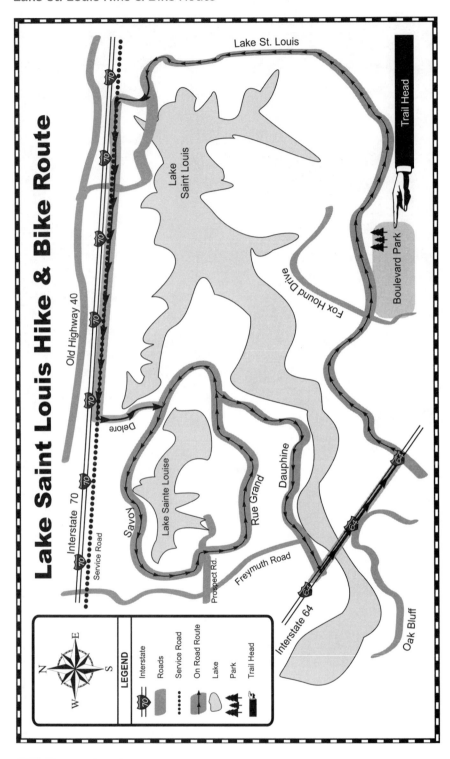

Lake Saint Louis Hike & Bike Route

Peggy Welch in the bike lane at Lake St. Louis.

Lake St. Louis Hike & Bike Route

Starting Point: Boulevard Park, Lake St. Louis, Missouri.

Directions to Starting Point: From St. Louis take Interstate 64/40 west to the Lake St. Louis Blvd. exit. Turn right (north) on Lake St. Louis Blvd. Boulevard park will be on the right about 0.9 mile.

Approximate Pedaling Time: 1-1.5 hours.

Distance: 10 miles.

Ride Description: From Boulevard Park turn right on to Lake St. Louis Blvd. The bike lane continues 2.5 miles, turn RIGHT on Bent Oak Cut-off Road. The bike lanes end here. Turn LEFT on the South Service Road. There is no bike lane here, there is a shoulder on the roadway. Turn LEFT on Deloire. This brings you to the inner loop that is marked with bicycle lanes. All the way around this loop is 2.9 miles. Turn RIGHT on Savoy. Savoy turns into Rue Grand. Continue on in the bike lane. Turn RIGHT on Dauphine. Continue on in the bike lane. At Hwy. 40 the bike lane ends. If you choose, turn around here and return to Boulevard Park the same way. The other option is to turn LEFT onto Hwy. 40. There are no bike lanes here, there is a shoulder on the road. Turn at the Lake St. Louis Blvd. exit and follow that back to Boulevard Park.

Things to See: This ride takes you through the Lake St. Louis development. On the ride you cross the dams on the lakes and some of the way has lake views.

Hazards: Traffic, gravel and debris in the bike lanes and on the shoulders of the roads. Parked cars in the bike lanes. Intersections with a lot of traffic.

Additional Thoughts: This is a nice ride if you live close by.

Terrain: Bike lanes on roadway and on-road riding. Some hills but they are not very steep.

Rating: Moderate.

Enjoying the view at Lake St. Louis.

WEST

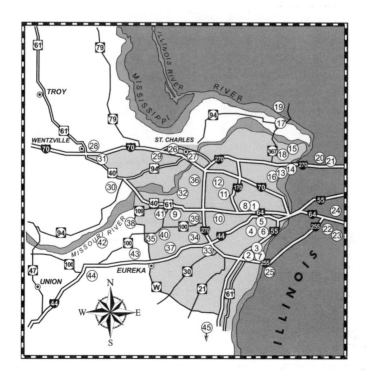

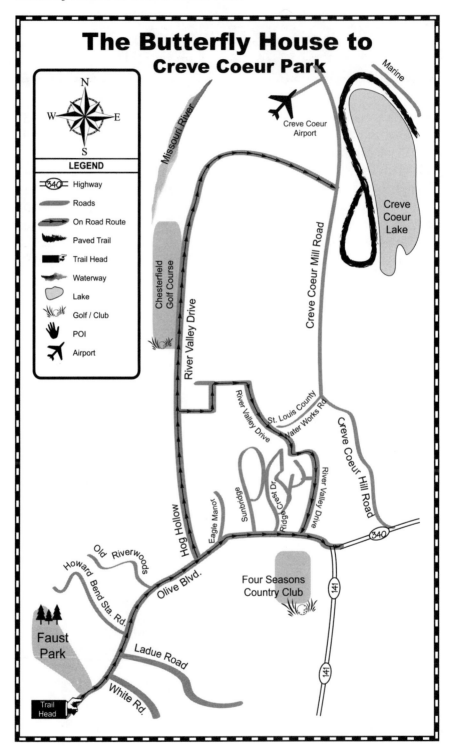

The Butterfly House to Creve Coeur Park

The Butterfly House to Creve Coeur Park Missouri River Valley Ride

Starting Point: Faust Park, Chesterfield, Missouri.

Directions to Starting Point: From St. Louis take Interstate 64/40 west to the Olive exit, turn right (north). Stay on Olive, the park will be on your left, approximately 1 mile.

Approximate Pedaling Time: 1.5-2 hours.

Distance: 15.5 miles. Add 5.5 miles if you ride the Creve Coeur Park bike path loop.

Ride Description: From Faust Park turn LEFT on to Olive. Go about 1.8 miles turn LEFT on to Hog Hollow road. Be cautious this is a steep downhill and the road is not in the best of shape. There is a very rough railroad track crossing at the bottom of the hill. Continue on Hog Hollow road. Continue straight on River Valley past the golf course and the old airport. In a few miles River Valley comes to Creve Coeur Mill Road. You can turn around here or go over to Creve Coeur Park and ride a lap of the bike path. That will add 5.5 miles to the ride. To go back, take River Valley back to the intersection by the golf course and turn left on River Valley. River Valley will curve around and then will go up a huge hill. Continue on to the stop at Olive. Turn RIGHT and continue on Olive to Faust Park.

Things to See: This ride begins on top of the Missouri River bluffs and travels down and through the Missouri River Bottoms. In Faust Park be sure to see the Sophia M. Sachs Butterfly House & Education Center. The Butterfly House features wonderful displays and a collection of 1,500 live butterflies. Faust Park is also the home of the St. Louis Carousel. The 1920 hand-carved Dentzel Carousel is still giving rides.

Hazards: Road hazards such as holes, bad pavement, railroad crossings, vehicle traffic. There are no shoulders on these roads. Traffic is lighter in the early morning.

Additional Thoughts: Call for times and fees for attractions.

Contact Info: Sophia M. Sachs Butterfly House & Education Center (636) 530-0076. Web site: www.butterflyhouse.org. St. Louis Carousel (636) 537-0222. Web site: www.stlouiscarousel.com.

Terrain: Mostly flat, with a big hill.

Rating: Moderate.

The Butterfly House features wonderful displays
and a collection of 1,500 live butterflies.

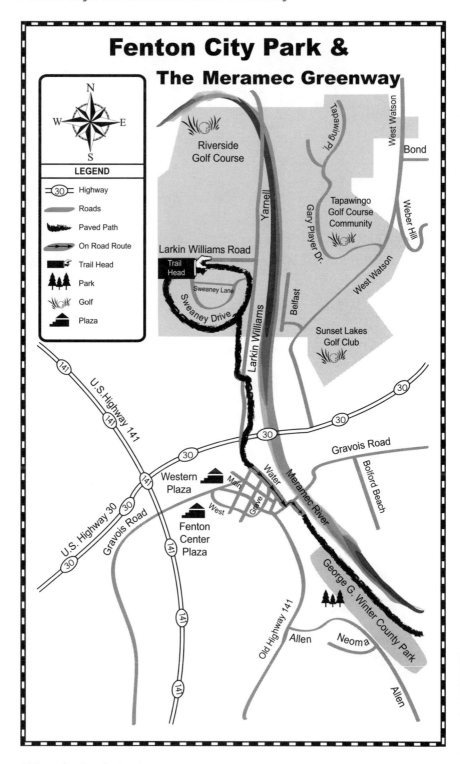

Fenton City Park
& the Meramec Greenway

Starting Point: Fenton City Park, Fenton, Missouri.

Directions to Starting Point: From St. Louis take Interstate 44 west. Immediately after crossing the Meramec River exit at the Soccer Park/North Highway exit. Immediately turn right on Soccer Park Drive. Turn right on Yarnell. Turn right at Sweaney Drive and into Fenton City Park.

Approximate Pedaling Time: 1-2 hours.

Distance: 5.5 miles.

Ride Description: Bicyclists, walkers, runners and rollerbladers share this paved trail. The trail begins in Fenton City park. To begin, travel around the loop in the park. Then the trail exits the park at the eastern end, crosses by Henderson Fields, and crosses Larkin Williams Road. The trail continues east along the Meramec River. At Mound Street the bike trail ends. Continue on-road east on Water Street to the Old Gravois road intersection. Cross Gravois and go a little northeast. Just before the old Gravois Bridge, turn east on Opps

Shortly after passing this scenic view of the Meramec River, the bike route continues on-road.—Photo by Cynthia Thompson.

Lane, by the Metropolitan Sewer District Plant. The trail cuts off to the left. There is a trail sign there. Continue on the trail to George Winter Park. Return the same way.

Things to See: Fenton is a town rich in history, well known for fossil finds and ancient Indian Petroglyphs. Fenton's historical river town buildings are just a short ride from the bicycle path. The Navajo Hotel and the Ice House are two main attractions of "Olde Towne." George Winter Park hosts a National Boat Race each summer.

Hazards: Watch for vehicle traffic when crossing roads and on the on-road section of this route. Sections of this route can flood.

Additional Thoughts: Drinking water and restrooms are available in Fenton City Park and George Winter Park. The paved trail sections make a good place to take kids to ride. This trail is part of the Meramec Greenway project.

Contact Info: City of Fenton Parks and Recreation, 645 New Smitzer Mill Road, Fenton, Missouri 63026. (636) 343-0067.

Terrain: Mostly flat with a few hills. Paved bicycle trail shared by runners and rollerbladers. A short section of this ride is on the road, without a bike lane.

Rating: Easy.

Location of the first bridge across the Meramec River in "Olde Towne" Fenton.
Some stone work of the original bridge can be seen at this site.
—Photo by Cynthia Thompson.

Simpson Park Bike Path

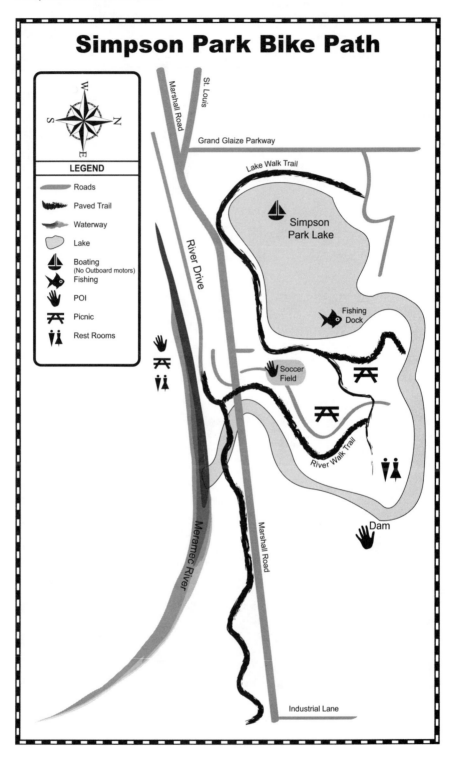

LEGEND

- Roads
- Paved Trail
- Waterway
- Lake
- Boating (No Outboard motors)
- Fishing
- POI
- Picnic
- Rest Rooms

Marshall Road

St. Louis

Grand Glaize Parkway

Lake Walk Trail

Simpson Park Lake

River Drive

Fishing Dock

Soccer Field

River Walk Trail

Meramec River

Marshall Road

Dam

Industrial Lane

Simpson Park Bike Path

Starting Point: There are two parking areas at Simpson Park. They are located on Grand Glaize Parkway and Marshall Road.

Directions to Starting Point: Simpson County Park is located in Valley Park off Marshall Road. To get there take Interstate 44 to the Hwy. 141 exit north. After about one-half mile on 141, make a right turn onto Marshall Road. The park entrance will be about a mile up the road on the left after going through the town of Valley Park.

Approximate Pedaling Time: 20 minutes to one hour depending on your speed.

Distance: 3.4 miles. The Lake Walk Trail is 0.8 mile. The River Walk Trail is 0.9 mile.

Ride Description: This is a paved path that is shared by bicyclists, walkers, runners and rollerbladers. The path is, for the most part, flat, with very small rises. The Lake Walk Trail is marked with red blazes and begins at the parking area located off Grand Glaize Parkway. The trail runs alongside the lake then connects to the River Walk Trail (yellow blazes) at the parking area located off of Marshall

Road. The River Walk Trail then crosses Marshall Road and continues along the Meramec River. The trail ends at the boundary of Kirkwood's Green Tree Park. If you wish to continue on, there is somewhat of a dirt park road you can ride on another 0.4 miles in dry conditions. In Green Tree Park there are restrooms, Bar-B-Q pits and picnic tables on the Meramec's banks.

Things to See: The Simpson Park Lake and the Meramec River attract a lot of wildlife. Flocks of geese are common, along with deer, and many species of birds. Woodpeckers keep busy in the wooded areas. Keep on the lookout for Great Blue Herons. We saw several on our visit. The large Blue Heron shelter has picnic tables, drinking fountains and trash cans. Fishing is allowed in the lake with a Missouri Fishing license. Boats without gas motors may be used. There is also a large playground for the kids to enjoy.

Hazards: This trail does get flooded by the Meramec River. Mud on the trail can be very slick. Do not attempt to swim or wade in the Meramec River. The river has strong currents and undertows.

A view of the Meramec River from the Simpson County Park Trail.

Additional Thoughts: Great views of the lake and the Meramec River. The park opens at 8 a.m. and closes one half hour after sunset. Restrooms are located near the Blue Heron Shelter. No swimming is allowed. Take your bug repellent. A good place to take the kids.

Contact Info: St. Louis County Parks Department, 41 S. Central Ave., Clayton, MO 63105. (314) 615-7275 (PARK).

Terrain: Flat paved trail that winds along the Meramec River.

Rating: Easy.

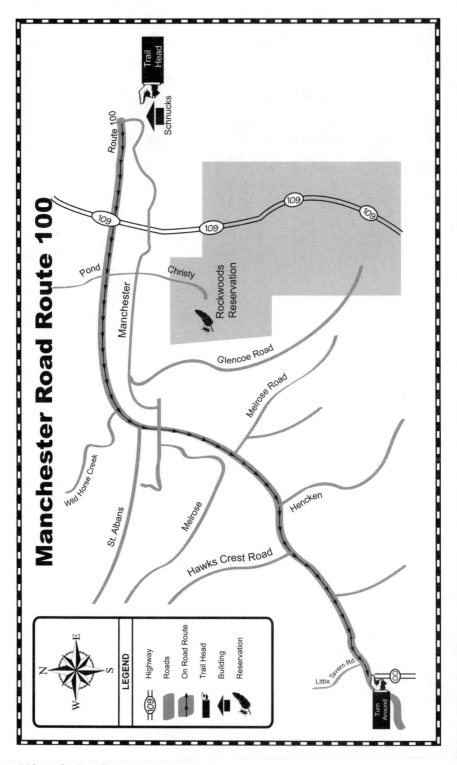

Manchester Road - Route 100

Starting Point: West St. Louis County, Wildwood Schnucks Market.

Directions to Starting Point: From Interstate 270 take Manchester Road west. Continue all the way out to Wildwood. Manchester Road changes its name to Route 100. If you continue straight, Manchester Road becomes Hwy. 100. Make a left turn to stay on Manchester (there's a Mobil Station on the southwest corner of the intersection) and park at the Schnucks Market on the left.

Approximate Pedaling Time: 1.5-2 hours

Distance: 20.8 miles out and back.

Ride Description: This is an on-road ride that goes along Route 100. The shoulder of the road is very wide. From the Schnucks parking lot, go back out to Route 100 and go west. Stay on Route 100 and go west until the Hwy. OO intersection. Turn around there and return the same way back to the Schnucks Market in Wildwood.

Things to See: Manchester Road was one of the earliest roads in the St. Louis area, dating back to 1816. This route takes you along a section of the historic Route 66 and the Lewis and Clark Trail. Today the road passes through the rolling hills of West St. Louis County.

Hazards: Road hazards. Cars. Watch for objects on the road, and holes. Glass and small pieces of rocks may give you flats.

Additional Thoughts: Tire liners such as "Spin skins" or "Mr. Tuffys" are recommended to prevent flat tires caused by debris on the road.

Terrain: Rolling hills, with some long, but not steep hills.

Rating: Moderate.

A dry winter ride on Manchester Road.

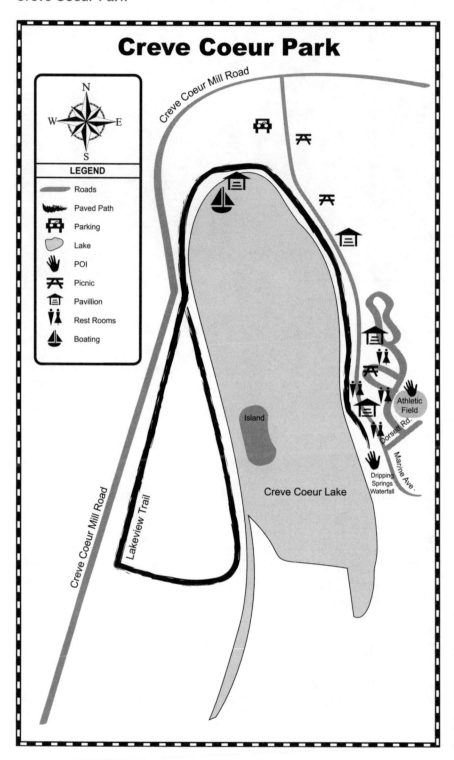

Creve Coeur Park

Creve Coeur Park Bike Path

Starting Point: Creve Coeur Park, Creve Coeur, Missouri.

Directions to Starting Point: From Interstate 270 take Dorsett Road west to Marine Ave. Make right turn, go approximately one-half mile. Bike path is on the left along lake. There are three parking lots along the paved bicycling path. Two are located off Marine Avenue. The other is located off of Creve Coeur Mill Road.

Approximate Pedaling Time: 45 minutes-1 hour.

Distance: 5.5-mile loop.

Ride Description: Bicyclists, walkers, runners and rollerbladers share this paved path. The path goes around the northern side of Creve Coeur Lake, with a loop at one end. It is mostly flat, with a few very slight ups and downs.

Things to See: Creve Coeur is French for "broken heart." Locally the legend is known of an Indian maiden who was "heart-broken" because her love, a French trapper, never returned. It is said that she cried tears that formed the lake in the shape of a heart, and then she drowned herself in it. Creve Coeur Lake was once a popular resort area. Around 1890, the resort was visited by thousands of St. Louisans on warm summer days. At one time, two hotels and many club houses were situated around the lake. There was an amusement park and more than 200 rowboats. Today one of the few remnants of the old days is the streetcar power house that sits up on the hill. The lake is now used for sailing and some fishing. Watch for birds and wildlife that visit the shore. Check out the waterfall located on the eastern side of the lake at the end of the bike path.

Hazards: Can get crowded on nice days. Some people don't keep their dogs on a leash. It is advised to walk bicycles over the small bridge. It can get very windy on some days.

Additional Thoughts: This wonderful park is a great place for a bike ride and a picnic with the kids. Water is available at drinking fountains during warm months. Restrooms are located on the east side of the lake off of Marine Ave. Closest bike shops are just a few miles away on Olive Street.

Contact Info: St. Louis County Parks Department, 41 S. Central Ave., Clayton, MO 63105. (314) 615-7275 (PARK).

Terrain: Paved bike path, mostly flat, a few slight ups and downs, one bridge that should be walked over.

Rating: Easy.

The path goes around the northern side of Creve Coeur Lake, with a loop at one end. It is mostly flat, with a few very slight ups and downs.

The famous Dripping Springs in Creve Coeur Park.—Photo by Cynthia Thompson.

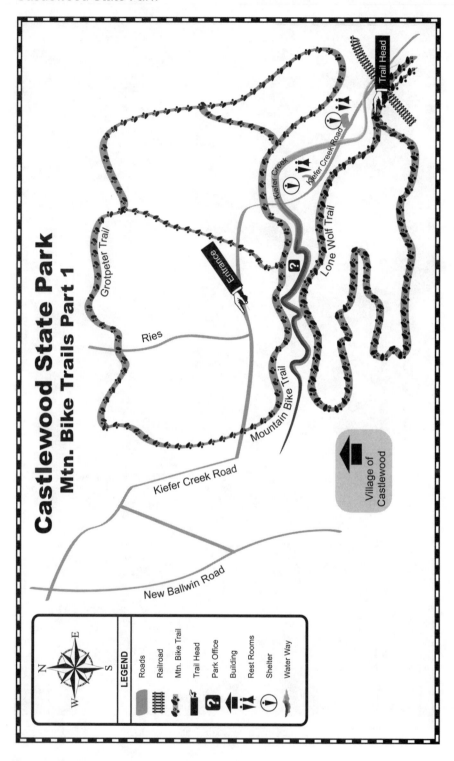

Castlewood State Park
Mtn. Bike Trails Part 1

Trail Head

Kiefer Creek Road

Kiefer Creek

Lone Wolf Trail

Grotpeter Trail

Entrance

Ries

Mountain Bike Trail

Kiefer Creek Road

New Ballwin Road

Village of Castlewood

N E S W

LEGEND

Roads
Railroad
Mtn. Bike Trail
Trail Head
Park Office
Building
Rest Rooms
Shelter
Water Way

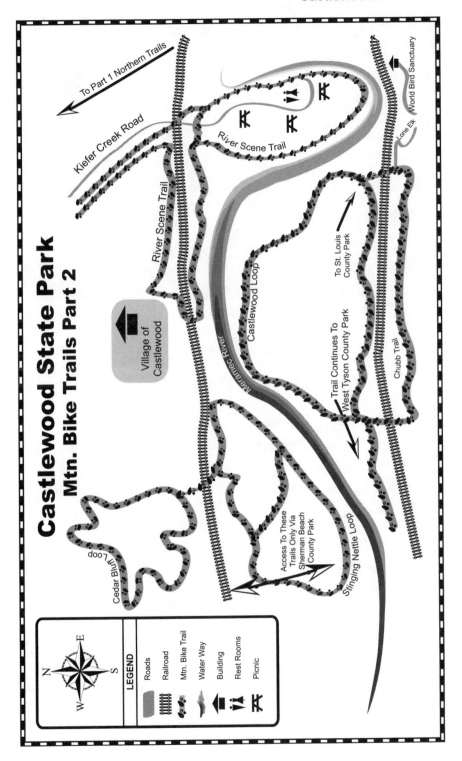

Access road to River Scene Trail in Castlewood State Park.—Photo by Cynthia Thompson.

Castlewood State Park
Mountain Bike Trails

Starting Point: Castlewood State Park, Ballwin, Missouri. (Because of washouts, some trails are not always accessible via Castlewood State Park. See below for directions to those trails.)

Directions to Starting Point: From Interstate 270 take Manchester Road west. Turn right on to New Ballwin Road. New Ballwin turns to the right and goes down a hill at the Oak road intersection. Turn left on Kiefer Creek Road and follow that into the park.

Due to the Meramec River washing out the access trail to Stinging Nettle Trail, the only trails accessible at this time from the entrance of Castlewood State Park are River Scene, Grotpeter, and Lone Wolf.

Directions to Stinging Nettle Trail/ Cedar Bluff Loop: From St. Louis take Manchester Road west past New Ballwin Road. At Kiefer Creek Road turn right. Turn right onto St. Paul Road. Follow St. Paul Road as it turns to the right. Turn left into the Sherman Beach County Park entrance. The trail is reached by parking at Sherman Beach County Park and taking the nature trail to Larry Elliot Road.

Directions to Chubb Trail/Castlewood Loop: Trailheads at Lone Elk Park & West Tyson County Park. **Lone Elk Park:** Take Interstate 44 west for 3 miles to the Valley Park exit (Hwy. 141). At the Valley Park exit, make a right turn (north) and then immediately turn right towards the North Outer Road. Turn left on the North Outer Road following signs to the Lone Elk County Park. **West Tyson County Park:** Trail starts at the Chubb Shelter in West Tyson County Park. Take I-44 to the Lewis Road exit. Turn right at the top of the ramp, left on Outer Road North, then right to the park.

Approximate Pedaling Time: 2 hours to all day.

Distance: There are 22.5 miles of trails for mountain biking.

> **River Scene Trail:** 3 mile loop, flat along the river.
> **Grotpeter Trail:** 3 mile loop, hilly.
> **Lone Wolf Trail:** 1.5 mile loop, hilly.
> **Stinging Nettle Trail:** 3 mile loop, flat with small dips and hills along river.
> **Cedar Bluff Loop:** 2 miles, hilly.
> **Chubb Trail:** 7 miles, one way.
> **Castlewood Loop:** 3 miles, it branches off of Chubb Trail.

Chubb Trail is hilly and rugged in West Tyson County before entering the river valley.

Ride Description: Dirt trail used by bicyclists and hikers. Start the ride at the large paved parking lot with the big pavilion. From here, head towards the river on the paved road. Just after passing under the railroad trestle watch for a trail on the left that cuts into the woods. Make a turn there and you are now on the River Scene Trail.

This three-mile loop is the most spectacular trail in the park and highlights the park's most memorable features. Watch for old foundations that were a part of the old hotels and club houses along this part of the trail.

The Lone Wolf Trail (1.5 miles) and the Grotpeter Trail (3 miles) are the toughest trails in the park. Both are hilly, rocky and technical. These trails travel through the wooded uplands of the park. The hills are tough climbs and the downhills can be technical. Take your time on the up hills and enjoy being out of doors.

The Stinging Nettle Loop is a three-mile loop, which circles through bottomland forest adjacent to the river. The area was the site for gravel dredging operations many years ago, so there are many ups and downs as you go through several large depressions. It is fairly easy to ride, but use caution on the technical sections along the river. Yes, the trail is named after the Stinging nettle plants that line the trail, and yes they do sting if you brush against them. Eventually this trail makes a loop.

At the very small creek crossing towards the end of the loop, the leg to the Cedar Bluff trail comes in. Locals call this the "Blue ribbon trail" because of the blue ribbons that were used to mark the trail when it was first cut. If you are up to the adventure of a 3-mile loop with some big hills make the turn and go through the tunnel under the railroad tracks.

You are now on the Cedar Bluff trail. Follow the trail markings and the loop will bring you back to the beginning. There are some great views from the hilltops. When riding this trail, I always find it hard to believe that I am still in the suburbs. Now back on the Stinging Nettles trail follow it back to Sherman Beach County Park.

Chubb Trail is a seven-mile trail that starts at the Chubb Shelter in West Tyson County Park. It passes through a part of Castlewood State Park and goes to the entrance of Lone Elk County Park. The trail is hilly and rugged in West Tyson County before entering the river valley. It passes two fields where prairie restoration areas are maintained by the St. Louis County Department of Parks and Recreation. The trail then becomes tightly wedged between a railroad embankment and the river. It widens as it enters the bottomland within Castlewood State Park before climbing one big hill to the entrance of Lone Elk County Park.

The Castlewood Loop is a three-mile trail that branches off Chubb Trail and further explores the bottomland of Castlewood State Park and the site of Lincoln Beach (swimming beach during the historic resort era.) The trail is very flat but it does offer excellent views of the Castlewood Bluff directly across the river. The trail is designated for hiking, bicycling, and equestrian use.

Things to See: The ride along the river is beautiful in all seasons. The flat trail is a good place to take kids mountain biking. Keep your eyes and ears open and you'll catch a glimpse of the kingfisher. This little bird dives into the water after its food. The Grand Staircase is located just off the Stinging Nettles Trail. During the early 1900s Castlewood was a resort area. The staircase guided vacationers from the trains up to the Hotels and cabins on top of the bluff.

Hazards: The trails along the river do flood. In the summer time the mosquitoes can be terrible, and watch for poison ivy. This park is very popular. Please be courteous to other trail users.

Additional Thoughts: Drinking water and restrooms are in the park and are open spring through fall. The park is open 7 a.m. to one-half hour after sunset (sharp!). Obey park speed limits—the rangers are very strict!

Contact Info: Castlewood State Park, 152 Keifer Creek Road, Ballwin, MO 63021. (636) 227-4433.

Terrain: Flat river bottoms and hilly upland forest.

Trail Status: Department of Natural Resources.

Rating: Moderate.

Cruising the trail at Castlewood State Park.

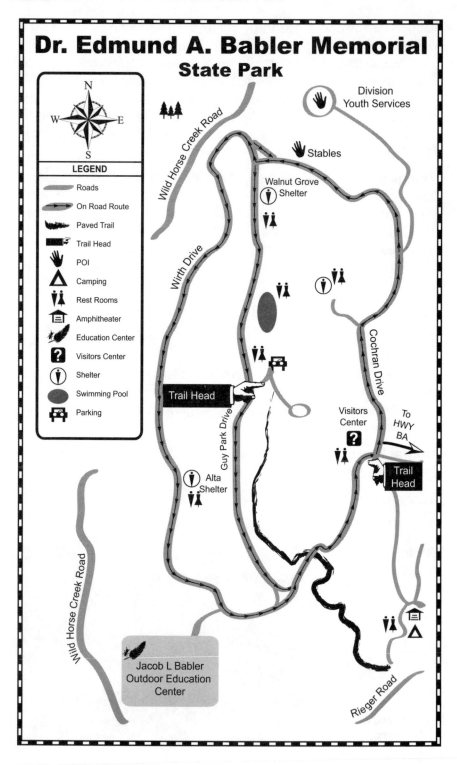

A bike race held at Babler Memorial State Park.

Dr. Edmund A. Babler Memorial State Park

Starting Point: Visitors Center, Dr. Edmund A. Babler Memorial Park, Wildwood, Missouri.

Directions to Starting Point: From St. Louis take Interstate 44 west to the Hwy. 109 exit. Go north on 109, out of Eureka, into Wildwood and continue past Hwy. 100. Be sure to stay to the left as it changes to Babler Park Road. Follow this to Guy Park Drive and the entrance to the park (left).

Approximate Pedaling Time: 30 minutes, to as long as you like.

Distance: 6 miles. There are several loop options: a 3.9-mile loop, a 4-mile loop, and a 4.5-mile loop, plus a 2-mile bike path that runs through the center of the park.

Ride Description: On-road and paved bike path. There are several on-road "loops." The east loop is four miles, the west loop is 3.9 miles. A ride around the outside of both loops would be 4.5 miles. Many people choose to ride multiple laps of this park because of the low traffic and the many hills.

Things to See: On August 20, 1930, Jacob L. Babler and his younger brother Henry gave 868 acres of land to the State of Missouri to be named the Dr. Edmund A. Babler Memorial State Park, after their brother. Much of the park was developed by the Civilian Conservation Corps (CCC). Jacob's support to the parks system earned him the title "Father of Missouri Parks." The visitors center contains many displays on the history of the park and the Bablers generosity and displays on the area's plants and animals. Oak, Hickory forest, deer, squirrels, wildflowers and woodpeckers are all over this park. The visitor center's displays show how the park came about and how the area's geology was formed. They have a model of the park, that shows the park's hills and land contours.

Hazards: Road hazards such as holes, debris and cars. Roads are slick when wet. Watch for deer crossing the roads.

Additional Thoughts: Great place if you want to ride hills. Not a good place to take the kids out to ride. The hills are just too big. Bicycles and mountain bikes are only permitted on paved trails and roads. Drinking water and restrooms available at the visitors center.

Contact Info: Dr. Edmund A. Babler Memorial State Park, 800 Guy Park Drive, Wildwood, MO 63005, (636) 458-3813.

Terrain: Very hilly.

Rating: Difficult.

Visitors Center at Babler Memorial State Park.

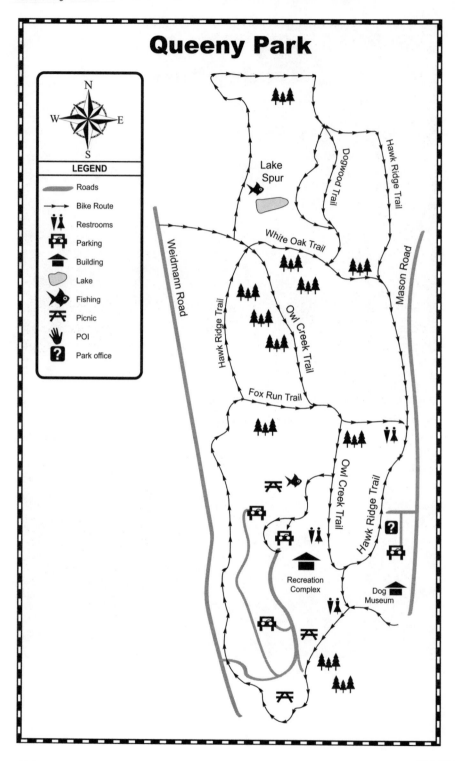

Queeny Park

LEGEND

Roads	
Bike Route	
Restrooms	
Parking	
Building	
Lake	
Fishing	
Picnic	
POI	
Park office	

Lake Spur

Dogwood Trail

Hawk Ridge Trail

Mason Road

White Oak Trail

Weidmann Road

Hawk Ridge Trail

Owl Creek Trail

Fox Run Trail

Owl Creek Trail

Hawk Ridge Trail

Recreation Complex

Dog Museum

Queeny Park

Starting Point: Edgar Queeny County Park, Ballwin, Missouri.

Directions to Starting Point: From Interstate 270 take Manchester Road west. Turn right on Weidman Road. The park is on the right.

Approximate Pedaling Time: 1 hour.

Distance: 7.8 miles of trails.

Ride Description: Consist of paved, dirt and gravel trails. You can start on the paved trail that goes up the hill behind the Rec Complex building. The trail curves around becoming dirt and gravel in some sections.

Things to See: There are several small lakes, creek crossings and mostly wooded areas. This urban park has quite a collection of wildflowers and wildlife.

Hazards: Many people use this park. Use caution and be courteous to other trail users. Take insect repellent.

Additional Thoughts: The trails are not marked very well, but this makes a great area to mountain bike that's not too difficult. Plus, even if you do get lost there are many people around to ask directions.

Contact Info: St. Louis County Parks Department, 41 S. Central Ave., Clayton, MO 63105. (314) 615-7275 (PARK).

Terrain: Somewhat hilly.

Rating: Moderate.

Ellisville Bike Trail

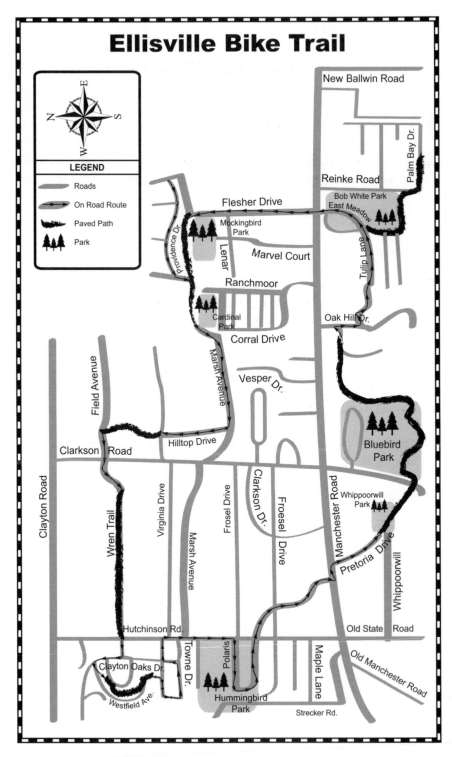

Ellisville Bike Trail

LEGEND

Roads

On Road Route

Paved Path

Park

New Ballwin Road

Palm Bay Dr.

Reinke Road

Bob White Park

East Meadow

Flesher Drive

Mockingbird Park

Providence Dr.

Lenar

Marvel Court

Tulip Lane

Ranchmoor

Cardinal Park

Oak Hill Dr.

Corral Drive

Marsh Avenue

Vesper Dr.

Field Avenue

Bluebird Park

Clarkson Road

Hilltop Drive

Clayton Road

Wren Trail

Virginia Drive

Marsh Avenue

Frosel Drive

Clarkson Dr.

Froesel Drive

Manchester Road

Whippoorwill Park

Pretoria Drive

Whippoorwill Road

Hutchinson Rd.

Old State Road

Clayton Oaks Dr.

Towne Dr.

Polaris

Maple Lane

Old Manchester Road

Westfield Ave.

Hummingbird Park

Strecker Rd.

Ellisville Bike Trail

Starting Point: Blue Bird Park, Ellisville, Missouri.

Directions to Starting Point: From Interstate 270 take Manchester Road west to Keifer Creek/ Clarkson Road intersection. Turn Left onto Keifer Creek Road. Turn left into Blue Bird park. The entrance driveway into the park is just across from the covered bridge.

Approximate Pedaling Time: 45 minutes-2 hours.

Distance: 7 miles.

Ride Description: On-road and bike path route. This 7-mile bike trail travels through five neighborhood parks. It begins at the covered bridge on Keifer Creek Road. The bike trail connects Blue Bird Park, Whippoorwill Park on the south side of Manchester Road, and on the north side of Manchester Road the trail connects Mocking Bird, Cardinal and Hummingbird Parks.

Things to See: There are two small covered bridges along this bike route. The creation of this trail was a first for the area. This trail was opened in 1975. Blue Bird park is the largest of the parks the path travels through. There you will find playgrounds, ball fields and a swimming pool.

Hazards: Part of this path is on-road, so be cautious of cars. The path also crosses Manchester Road, use caution when crossing this busy road.

Additional Thoughts: Although the City of Ellisville calls this a bike trail, much of the route is on roads. The only special signs are at the crossings at Manchester Road and where the on-road route returns to a trail. Bike shops are just a short distance away. Drinking water and restrooms are available at Blue Bird park. This would be a fun ride to take along a picnic lunch.

Contact Info: City of Ellisville, 1 Weis Ave, Ellisville, MO 63011. (636) 227-9660.

Terrain: Paved bicycle path and on-road route with rolling hills.

Rating: Moderate.

FAR WEST & BEYOND

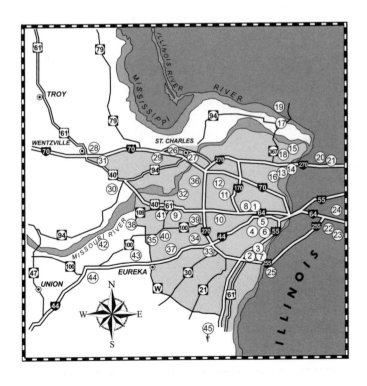

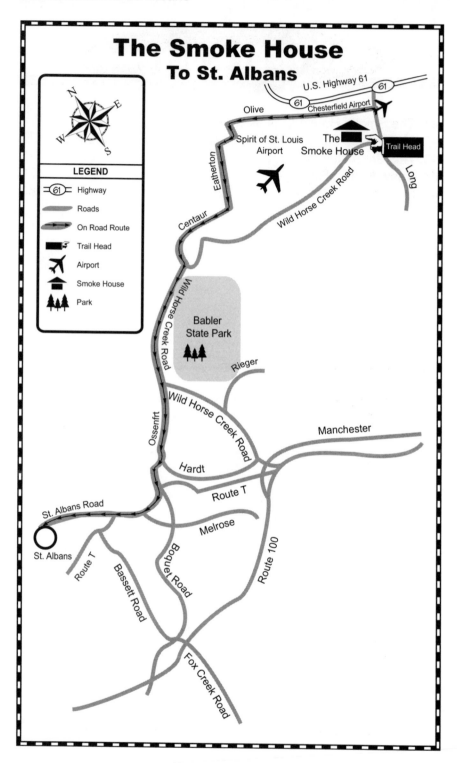

The Smoke House
To St. Albans

The Smoke House to St. Albans

Starting Point: The Smoke House Restaurant and Market, Chesterfield, Missouri.

Directions to Starting Point: From St. Louis take Interstate 64/40 west to the Chesterfield Parkway exit 19 A. This exit is after the Olive/Clarkson Road exit. At the light turn right on Chesterfield Airport Road. Turn right onto Baxter Road. Turn left back onto Chesterfield Airport Road to the Smoke House.

Approximate Pedaling Time: 3.5-4.5 hours.

Distance: 33 miles.

Ride Description: On-road ride out to the St. Albans area and back. Cycle west on Chesterfield Airport Road. LEFT on Olive Road, it jogs to the right by the gas station. LEFT on Eatherton Road. RIGHT on Centaur Road. RIGHT on Wildhorse Creek. RIGHT on Ossenfort and up hill. RIGHT on St. Albans Road (Hwy. T), down big hill. RIGHT on St. Albans road, continue until you see Head's Store, a yellow and green two-story building. Stop for snacks and/or a sandwich at the store. Return the same way.

Things to See: Watch along Wildhorse Creek Road for the Old Bethel Methodist Church. The Church is a stone building dating to 1859. Heads Store in St. Albans is a famous cycling landmark.

Hazards: Road hazards such as traffic, holes, gravel on road. There is no shoulder to ride on and the continuing growth of this area brings more and more traffic.

Additional Thoughts: This is one of the most popular rides for cyclists in the area.

Terrain: Somewhat flat with two big hills.

Rating: Difficult.

The picturesque 1859 Bethel Church on Wild Horse Creek.

Stop in for a cool drink or a homemade sandwich to re-energize you on the ride back. Photo by Cynthia Thompson.

Mae Head's Store & Saint Albans, Missouri

Founded by Peter Kincaid in 1837, St. Albans was settled mostly by Germans. The quaint yellow and green framed buildings of the town sit at the foot of the hills of the Missouri River Valley nicknamed the "Rhineland of Missouri" for the area's similarity to Germany's wine country.

Not far from town flows the "Mighty" Missouri River that brought the Corps of Discovery expedition to a small cave just north of town. It was here at Tavern Cave that Meriwether Lewis nearly fell to his death while exploring the cave. He slipped and fell nearly 20 feet before he caught himself by digging his knife into a crevice.

St. Albans is home to Head's Store, another cycling icon of the area. The store is owned and operated by Mae Head. Mae was born and raised in St. Albans. She bought the store in 1942 from her father. He had purchased the store in 1915.

One big ride sticks in Mae's memory, the time 400 riders visited during an organized ride. Now that's a lot of sandwiches! Mae enjoys collecting dolls as you will see. She'll be happy to show you where the water of the flood of '93 came up to the window sills. With the help of over 30,000 sandbags, the store survived the great flood.

The store opened in 1892. A photo of the original store and the owners hangs across from the famous sandwich counter. Stop in for a tasty homemade sandwich. You will enjoy the visit!

The Greensfelder Road Ride

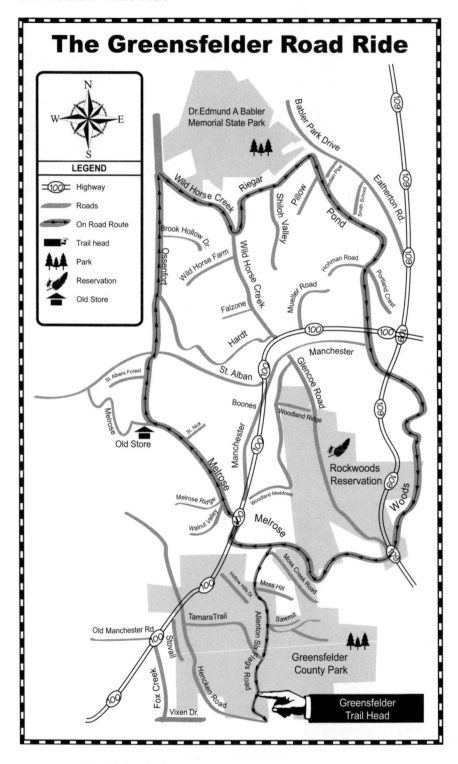

On the Greensfelder Ride you can lose yourself amid the quiet, pastoral scenery.

The Greensfelder Road Ride

Starting Point: The Learning Center, A.P. Greensfelder County Park, Eureka, Missouri.

Directions to Starting Point: From St. Louis take Interstate 44 west to the Allenton Six Flags Road exit. Take Allenton Six Flags Road north. The entrance to the Learning Center parking lot will be on the right, watch for the sign.

Approximate Pedaling Time: 2-3 hours.

Distance: 22.8 miles.

Ride Description: This on-road route begins at the Learning Center parking lot in A. P. Greensfelder County Park. Turn RIGHT (north) onto Allenton Six Flags road out of the parking lot. At stop sign turn RIGHT onto Melrose. After the big downhill section, stay to the right at the fork in the road. Cross 109 and continue straight on Woods Road. At the top of the hill turn LEFT onto Old Manchester Road. Cross 109 and continue on Old Manchester Road. Turn RIGHT onto Pond. Follow Pond across 100 to Rieger Road. Turn LEFT onto

Rieger Road. Turn RIGHT onto Wild Horse Creek. At bottom of steep hill turn LEFT (use caution) onto Ossenfort. Stay on Ossenfort up big hill and across St. Albans Road (Hwy. T). Turn LEFT onto Melrose. The Kreienkamp Store is the large white building. Stay on Melrose back to Route 100. Turn RIGHT onto Route 100 a short distance and turn LEFT onto Melrose/Allenton Six Flags Road. At the stop sign turn RIGHT onto Allenton Six Flags Road and follow that back to the Learning Center Parking lot in Greensfelder Park.

Things to See: This ride takes you through some of the most scenic spots between Greensfelder Park and Rockwoods Reservation. In the winter you can see Hidden Valley Ski Resort with its snow-covered ski runs on the hillsides. The ride will take you past the Kreienkamp Store in what, at one time, was the town of Melrose. Built around 1854 it was operated by the same family until 1978. Today it is a private residence.

Hazards: Use caution on the large downhills. Watch for road hazards such as traffic, holes, gravel, and debris on the roadway. Watch for deer crossing the roads and watch for dogs.

Additional Thoughts: Nice mid-range ride for the road bike enthusiast.

Terrain: Some large hills.

Rating: Difficult.

As always, pay attention to the road signs.

Jen Goldstein, left, and Karen Johnson pedal past
the Kreienkamp Store on Melrose Road.

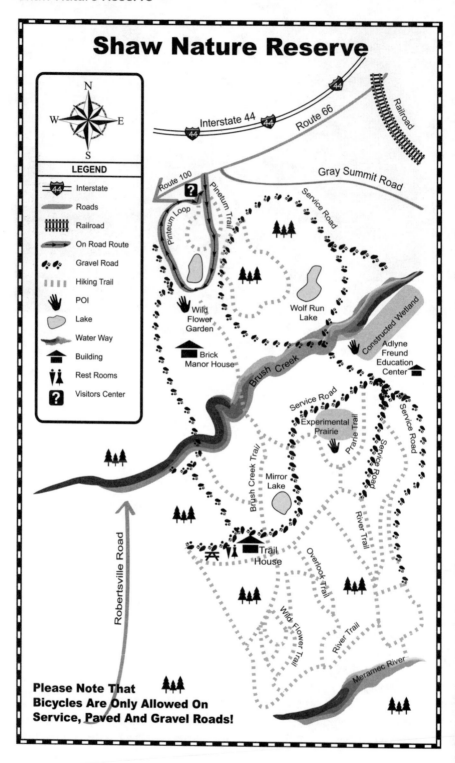

Shaw Nature Reserve

Please Note That Bicycles Are Only Allowed On Service, Paved And Gravel Roads!

Much of the Shaw Nature Reserve is off limits to cyclists, but there are still more than eight miles of gravel service roads and the Pinetum Loop to enjoy.

Shaw Nature Reserve

Starting Point: Shaw Nature Reserve Visitors Center.

Directions to Starting Point: The Shaw Nature Reserve (formerly known as Shaw's Arboretum) is located in Gray Summit, 22 miles from Interstate 270. Take Interstate 44 west to the Gray Summit exit 233. Turn left over the overpass, make right turn at outer road (Hwy 100). The nature reserve is on the left.

Approximate Pedaling Time: 1 hour-2.5 hours.

Distance: 8 miles of gravel roads.

Ride Description: Bicycles are only allowed on paved roads and gravel roads. Maps are available at the Visitors Center along with many guides to the wildlife and fauna you will see at the reserve.

Things to See: One of the first things you will see are the Cypress trees along Pinetum Lake. The Whitmire Wildflower Gardens are a recommended stop during spring and summer. The gardens contain many wildflowers and each one is labeled, identifying the plant.

Your ride will also take you to the Experimental Prairie area. The summer is an exceptionally wonderful time to see the prairie in bloom and the native prairie grasses at their peak. A short hike up the Prairie

Trail leads you to an observation deck with a panoramic view of the prairie. Watch for hawks and other birds. Another point worth a short hike is the Constructed Wetlands Area. A three-quarter mile walk brings you to the constructed wetlands area. There is a viewing stand "blind" on the western end of the lake where you can watch birds, deer, and maybe catch a glimpse of the beavers. A boardwalk actually goes out into the wetlands area for an up close view of the plants and animals. The bench on the boardwalk provides a prime place to see fish, frogs, dragon flies and the beautiful lilies.

Hazards: Be cautious on the gravel roads. It is easy to take a spill on them. Bring bug spray to repel ticks, mosquitoes and the normal summer pests.

Additional Thoughts: There is a fee to get into the Shaw Nature Reserve if you are not a member of the Missouri Botanical Gardens. As of this writing, the fee for adults is $3.00, a Missouri Botanical Gardens membership is $60 for a family, and a Shaw Nature Reserve only membership is $30. Restrooms, drinking water and picnic areas are located at the Visitors Center and Trail House pavilion.

Contact Info: Shaw Nature Reserve, P.O. Box 38, Gray Summit, MO 63039. (636) 451-3512.

Terrain: Gravel roads rolling hills.

Rating: Moderate.

Watch out for the blood-sucking butterflies. They can sense fear.

Although not open for cyclists, be sure and leave
time for a walk along the wetlands trail.

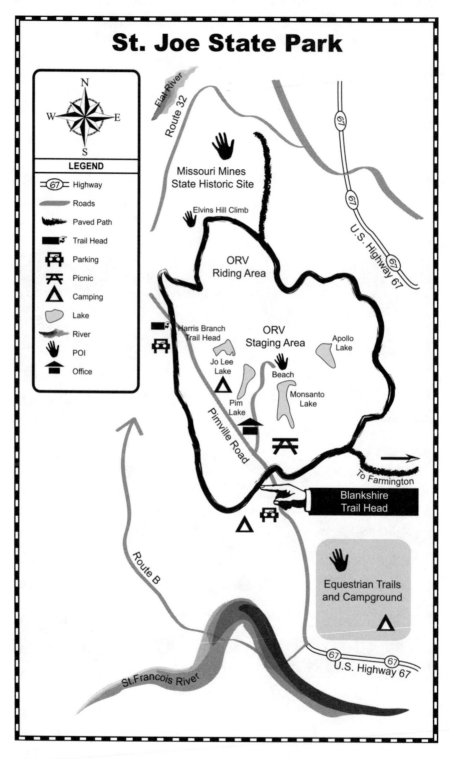

St. Joe State Park Bike Path

Starting Point: St. Joe State Park, Flat River, Missouri.

Directions to Starting Point: From St. Louis take Interstate 55 south to Festus. At Festus, take U.S. Hwy. 67 south to the Leadington/ Park Hills exit. Turn right onto Hwy. 32 west and travel about 3.5 miles before turning left onto Pimville Road (just before the railroad tracks). Parking is available at the two trailheads located off of Pimville Road.

Approximate Pedaling Time: 1-2 hours.

Distance: A little over 14 miles of paved trails.

Ride Description: This paved bike trail, with its steep and rolling hills is a favorite getaway for many bicyclists. Located in the St. Francis mountain area the park setting offers great views of the forest and rolling hills. The Harris Branch and Blankshire trail heads are located along Pimville Road. Other trail accesses are located at the Pim day-use area, Missouri Mines State Historic Site, and most recently opened, the Farmington trail head. This allows access to and from the city of Farmington, about 1.25 miles away.

The portion of the trail north of Pimville Road is eight miles in length; the portion south of Pimville Road is three miles in length. The spur connecting the Pim day-use area to the bicycle trail is 0.6 miles in length and fairly level. The half-mile spur connecting Missouri Mines State Historic Site to the northern portion of the bicycle trail is also mostly level. The newest section of the trail that connects the bicycle trail at approximately the 1.5 mile marker to the new trail head is 1.7 miles long.

Lakeview Trail is a 1.5-mile loop that can be accessed from the Pim day-use area or from the Monsanto Lake area. It is paved for 0.2 mile. The rest of the trail is both level and steep, and is earthen and rocky. This trail is for use by walkers and mountain bicyclists.

Things to See: Beautiful wooded park land in the St. Francis Mountains. The park is on what use to be mines that were operated by the St. Joe Lead Company. Many miles of mine shafts run underground. A mining museum is located at the north end of the park. This section of Missouri is often referred to as the "Lead Belt." At one time most of the world's lead was mined here. The path passes three lakes that are filled with cattails and visited by lots of wildlife.

Hazards: Take plenty of water and bug spray.

Additional Thoughts: This makes a fun getaway adventure weekend. Camping is available in the park. Water is available from April through October at the Blankshire trail head and at the Pim day-use area. Vault toilets are located at the Blankshire trail head, the Harris Branch trail head and the Pim day-use area. Part of the park is designated for off-road vehicle use and is visited by many motorcyclists each year. Elephant Rocks State Park is close by.

Contact Info: Missouri State Parks at 1 (800) 334-6946.

Terrain: Paved bicycle path with rolling and some steep hills.

Rating: Moderate.

Bibliography

City of Ellisville. Compiled and edited by Carolyn Jolly Pratt, Dolores M. Kaemmerer, Sondra J. Murphy, Victor Reinke.

Curtis, C. H. (Skip). *The Missouri Route 66 Tour Book.* Curtis Enterprises, 1994.

Dufur, Brett. *The Complete Katy Trail Guidebook.* Pebble Publishing, 2002.

Dufur, Brett. *Show Me Mountain Biking.* Pebble Publishing, 1999.

Fanselow, Julie. *Traveling the Lewis and Clark Trail.* Falcon Publishing, 1999.

Fifield, Barringer and Keith Recker. *Seeing Beyond Saint Louis.* Washington University Campus Stores, 1991.

Henry, Steve. *The Mountain Biker's Guide to the Ozarks.* Menasha Ridge Press and Falcon Press, 1993.

Kodner, Barbara. Olivette: *Chronicle of a Country Village.* The Patrice Press, 1979.

Meyer, Duane, Ph.D. *The Heritage of Missouri-A History.* State Publishing Co., Inc., 1965.

Rothwell, Dan A. *A Guide to Chesterfield's Architectural Treasures.* 1998.

Rubright, Robert. *Walks and Rambles in and around St. Louis.* Backcountry Publications, 1995.

Wildwood a Great Beginning. 1997.

Author & Photographer Margo Carroll

About the
Author & Photographer

Margo Carroll has been a photographer for as long as she can remember. She says what drives her is the enjoyment she gets sharing what she sees with others.

Margo has raced bikes since she was 14, including BMX, road and mountain bikes—and has been ranked number 2 nationally.

"I enjoy mostly just riding, enjoying the sights, sounds and smells of the forest. Mountain biking is such a wonderful experience, it can take you places you will never see in a car. I enjoy riding in all the different seasons and enjoying the wildflowers or the quiet crispness of a winter day," Margo said.

Margo was also one of the founders of the Midwest Mountain Bike Club, back in the 1980s This group was the first of its kind in this area and was instrumental in establishing mountain biking relationships with area land managers, and bringing people together. The Club also promoted a 12-race series each year and the State Championships for several years.

Margo founded and is very involved with the Women's Riding Network, a group of women who cycle in the St. Louis area. She is also a sales representative at Riteway Products, a division of GT. Her photography is featured in Brett Dufur's book *Show Me Mountain Biking,* including the cover. *Cycling St. Louis* is her first book.

Throughout her work and play, her goal remains the same. "I enjoy sharing the great joys of cycling with others. As Ghandi said, "We must be the change we wish to see in the world.' "

REDUCE, REUSE, RECYCLE

In creating this book, many steps were taken to reduce paper waste. Computers now make "paperless" offices a semi-reality. Paper scrap and early drafts of this book were recycled, and the paper stock for this book is 20 percent pre-consumer waste.

Websites
for Rainy Day
Armchair Odysseys

Cyber Cyclery Internet Biking Hub: http://cyclery.com

Department of Natural Resources:
www.state.mo.us/dnr/dsp/homedesp.htm

Earthriders Mountain Bike Club Web Site. Kansas City based:
www.earthriders.org,

Hostelling International/AYH: www.gatewayhiayh.org/

Interactive Katy Trail: www.katytrail.showmestate.com

Missouri Conservation Department Website:
www.conservation.state.mo.us

Missouri online highways: www.ohwy.com/mo/homepage.htm

More state park information: www.mostateparks.com
This site includes descriptions and good maps for every state
park and historic site in Missouri.

The Nature Conservancy (Official): http://nature.org/

Ozark Trail Site:
http://slluez.home.mindspring.com/transozarktrail.html

Outdoor Activities in the St. Louis Area:
www.explorestlouis.com/attractions

Outdoor Guide Magazine: www.outdoorguidemagazine.com

Order Midwest guidebooks online: www.pebblepublishing.com

Quick access to MTNF campground information:
www.gorp.com/dow/eastern/mtw.htm

TC Tours: www.touringcyclist.com

RIDE LOG:

Date: Trail Name:

Weather:

List of Riders:

How Long it Takes to Get There:

Comments:

Next Time Bring:

Date: Trail Name:

Weather:

List of Riders:

How Long it Takes to Get There:

Comments:

Next Time Bring:

RIDE LOG:

Date: Trail Name:

Weather:

List of Riders:

How Long it Takes to Get There:

Comments:

Next Time Bring:

Date: Trail Name:

Weather:

List of Riders:

How Long it Takes to Get There:

Comments:

Next Time Bring:

RIDE LOG:

Date:　　　　Trail Name:

Weather:

List of Riders:

How Long it Takes to Get There:

Comments:

Next Time Bring:

Date:　　　　Trail Name:

Weather:

List of Riders:

How Long it Takes to Get There:

Comments:

Next Time Bring: